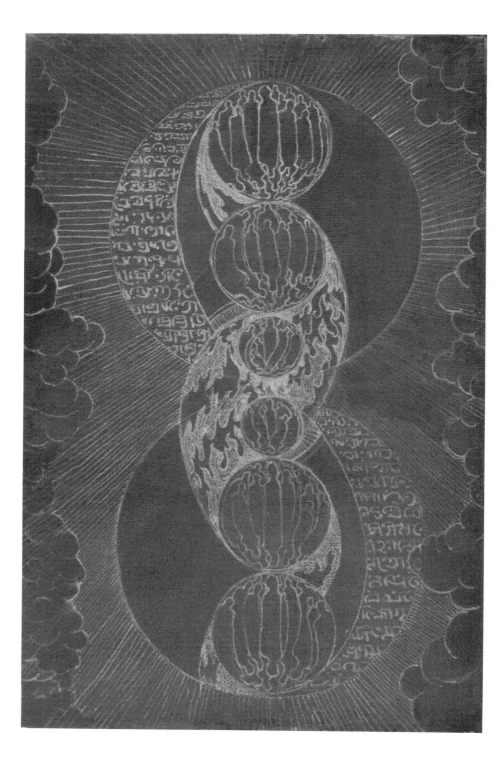

THE NEW
(REATION
STORY

Spirit, Eros, & Climate Chaos

TRILOGY BY
ANDREW F. BEATH

BOOK ONE

ISBN: 0615927963

ISBN 13: 9780615927961

Library of Congress Control Number: 2013922167

New Epoch Books, Malibu, CA

DEDICATION AND ACKNOWLEDGMENTS

My friend Bob Chartoff, the well-respected producer of more than forty major motion pictures, has been a confidant for many years; as such, he has indirectly and unknowingly provided insight and encouragement that has helped me to write this manuscript. I dedicate these pages to Bob. In addition, my two young children are always an inspiration. Leonardo is now ten years old, and AnaSophia is eight. I would like to also dedicate this work to them and to their young contemporaries around the globe who face an uncertain future.

During the late 1970s and early 1980s, Dr. Cynthia Mathis Beath was my traveling companion. We explored more than sixty countries together, including exotic destinations such as Africa's Serengeti Plains, Tibet's monasteries, and Bali's artistic countryside. She helped me understand the world's mysteries from new perspectives, both physical and spiritual. Cynthia has been a professor at several major universities. Upon finishing the manuscript for *Book One, In the Beginning*, but prior to doing an edit, I sent it to Cynthia to read. Within a short time, without being asked, she returned a detailed edit, which I assiduously utilized for a rewrite and refinement of these pages. The book is much better as a result. What a gift! Thank you.

Janet Harrington and Jay Levin read the manuscript and provided helpful edits and insightful comments. Thank you both. Other friends read the manuscript and helped to make it better, including Gilbert Levy, Aaron Kipnis, and Eric Seifert. My thanks go out to them for their selfless contributions.

Leigh J. McCloskey provided the images used for the Book's interior. He is a visionary artist and philosopher. Leigh is a modern renaissance man. He has deeply explored the archetypal and hidden aspects of the psyche through his visual art works and writing. The works that are included here come from Leigh's *Codex Tor* illuminated books and *Grimoire* (Book of Spells). Robert Swedroe created the image opposite the appendixes, which is also *Book Two*'s cover. Steve Chapple took the author's photo that appears on the back cover.

I am grateful to Rafael Lopez for the book cover's beautiful artwork. The artist can be contacted at: Rafael López Studio, 843 Tenth Avenue Studio C, San Diego CA 92101, ph. 619.237.8061, website www.rafael-lopez.com

TABLE OF CONTENTS

Preface · xiii

Introduction · xv

Chapter 1   Changing Our Worldview Changes the World · · · · · · · · · 1

Chapter 2   The Grand Perspective: Who Am I,
            and What Am I Doing Here? · · · · · · · · · · · · · · · · · 25

Chapter 3   The Cosmos Bursts Forth · · · · · · · · · · · · · · · · · 57

Chapter 4   In the Beginning · 75

Chapter 5   Creation Stories and Human Culture · · · · · · · · · · · · 111

Chapter 6   From Hominids to Homo sapiens · · · · · · · · · · · · · 125

Chapter 7   Tools, Fire and Language ·151

Chapter 8   Natural Harmony ·169

Chapter 9   God: The Great Mystery ·195

Chapter 10 Concluding Thoughts: The Human Experiment · · · · · · 223

Appendixes · 249

Bibliography · 259

BOOK ONE

IN THE BEGINNING

PREFACE

I'm writing this preface after rereading the introduction and chapter 1 for the first time since a recent edit. I realize that I am asking a lot of you, the reader, because there are many concepts included here that are likely to be new to you and might seem somewhat perplexing. This is a creation story; it is linear but not linear, logical but not logical. For the most part, the presentation is curvilinear and organic, with rounded edges (like Nature). Because the book's gestalt is circular, you can be assured of reencountering the unfamiliar in a different form as the story unfolds; through various perceptual approaches, you will eventually "see" the zeitgeist that is being presented.

That is not to say that you will necessarily agree with everything you find in these pages; I do not expect that—the story is too new and far-reaching. My hope is to catalyze alternative ways for you to perceive the world and its most profound realities. Your new perspective will not be the same as the worldview presented here, and it may not necessarily agree with these philosophies. Perhaps you will discover your own creation story. It may be similar to this one or entirely different. I would be happy with either result.

Please read with an open mind and open heart. If a concept seems vague or not readily comprehensible, just move past it without missing a beat; don't let it slow you down. There will be more meaningful information, ideas, and philosophies showing up a few pages later. All the difficult information is covered in both intuitive and logical forms; thus, the worldview presented becomes more and more familiar as one explores these pages. When you encounter an unfamiliar concept, don't let it interrupt your reading flow; just let it go by, like a stick floating under a bridge in the stream of life. By the last chapter, the seemingly complex will be shown to be, in actuality, rather simple.

Our story incorporates the fascinating contrast between "right-brain" and "left-brain" functions; this plays into masculine and feminine values and strengths, especially "rational mind" and "intuitive mind." I have written most of the technical, scientific, research-oriented, and explanatory material in regular text with normal margins. The more intuitive, spiritual, speculative, metaphysical, philosophical, and poetic parts of our New Creation Story are italicized and indented. This is the more feminine voice speaking, which comes from "wisdom guide" Sophia. This presentation gives both the logical and the magical equal human influence and attempts to show how they are able to dance and play in heart-full unity; indeed, this coming together is a prerequisite if our world is to survive without being torn asunder. Thank you for embarking on this adventure with me. I am honored by your presence.

INTRODUCTION

In the past one hundred years a new planetary danger
has arisen. The Earth bleeds on the cross of human
industry. This system uses people as fuel. It is an engine
of competition that consumes the delicate fibers of our
compassionate connections to all life.[1]

This three-book trilogy offers a new look at the human condition through the prism of a Creation Story. Where did we come from, and who are we as a species in this present moment on Earth? The story is a multidisciplined tapestry that begins with our Universe's cosmic birth and extends through human evolution, redefining the human condition based on recently revealed scientific and intuitive wisdom.

In our Creation Story, there is a "cosmological imperative" that drives both biological evolution and the evolution of human consciousness. Ever since *Homo sapiens* emerged from earlier hominids about two

---

1 Andrew Beath, *Consciousness in Action* (New York, NY) Lantern Press, 2006).

hundred thousand years ago, human consciousness has been continuously evolving. As it evolves from one stage to the next, it produces more profound "epochs" that result in changed human behavior on both individual and cultural levels. This evolution of human consciousness has recently reached a new plateau that offers us an expanded worldview. These books describe how this new perspective differs from the prevailing cultural way of seeing the world.

I incorporate the latest hard science, including quantum mechanics, cosmology, anthropology, life origins, biological evolution, and medicine. We also delve into the more subjective disciplines, including philosophy, religion, and spirituality, among others. As such, the story is an amalgam of science, philosophy, and metaphysics: science represents human knowledge at this moment in our evolutionary development; philosophy invites mind-play; and metaphysics provides a spiritual dimension.

Interconnection and joy are more deeply felt when we realize our interdependence. Affiliation and intimacy become more accessible. The conceptual grounding for this process is a notion that I call "Natural Harmony." My definition is "the mutually beneficial reciprocity woven into the web of life, which has allowed life on Earth to endure and evolve over billions of years." Natural Harmony is the thread we follow in weaving our story.

In this New Creation Story, we "see" how evolving consciousness transforms human spirituality, and how this expanding awareness affects individuals as well as entire societies. We learn why we are currently "out of tune" with Natural Harmony—our sacred Earth community—and examine what is needed to rectify this imbalance. Enhanced consciousness expands one's capacity to access spirit. The bonding force among all things large and small is Eros; the personal, interactive one-to-one connecting force is love. Eros, love, and beauty reside within all living things, making up their core essence and ideal form. Natural Harmony is the planetwide relationship that connects individual entities at their core. As a person's connection to spirit is strengthened, his or her life experience is imbued with intimacy, meaning, and joy.

Our story plumbs humanity's most profound theories and imaginings: the cosmos, life's origins, humans' emergence, life's meaning, love, Eros, and intimacy. "What is God?" The many answers to this question are not subject to intellectual verification; however, like all *Homo sapiens* before us, we continue to ponder and speculate about the Creative Source, deepening human consciousness in the process. This story addresses the transpersonal realms in its many forms: the Divine, the Creative Source, God, Goddess, Sacred Nature, and Great Spirit, among others. We learn how these concepts help us navigate within our current conundrum. Naturally, our story contains a spiritual worldview; however, it is not at odds with either science or with Christianity, Judaism, Islam, or the other major religions. On the contrary, it is developed from all that has ever been revealed, no matter what tradition or discipline.

Spiritual forms emerge from the evolution of human consciousness. Religions are born out of a culture's consciousness. The Divine takes many forms, each one molded from the consciousness epoch in which it is held. Broad consciousness categories are stages; an individual's consciousness may be considered a "state" within a stage. Entire cultures are typically confined to a particular state of consciousness. These ideas will be examined in detail as our New Creation Story unfolds.

This trilogy calls on us to expand our own consciousness. In my own life, starting in my late twenties, I had a burning desire to better understand the world, to travel, to explore, to investigate various religions and mystical phenomena. So, at age thirty, I left a corporate job and began to travel. This globe-hopping lasted for ten years and involved visits to eighty countries, resulting in a transformed worldview. Then, at age forty, I started the not-for-profit organization called EarthWays. Although it had taken a full decade, my life was totally changed.

and the day came
when the risk
to remain tight in the
bud was more painful
than the risk it took
to blossom

—Anaïs Nin

Cultures have masculine and feminine qualities and characteristics, as do individuals. One is often out of balance with the other. These imbalances define how a society treats its citizens and how it behaves toward neighboring communities. The flux in this balance over many thousands of years is an important variable in understanding human history and explaining social structures such as person-to-person relationships, gender equality, each group's attitude toward those who are different, human interactions with Nature, spiritual development, philosophy, and all other cultural activities. The human part of this story weaves a dance between the genders, including a look at the first-ever coming together between the Divine Feminine and the Enlightened Masculine.

The Ecological Crisis

By virtue of our mental genius and our rapacious appetite for "stuff," we humans have become a most integral part of an interdependent Earth community. The Earth is withering. Paradoxically, as the destruction expands, we are discovering how to live sustainably and to protect the beauty that remains all around us.

In these violent and challenging times, human interaction with Nature has become of utmost importance. This marriage is in critically ill health. Curing this condition, making it healthy once again, is the most important challenge of our era. The forests with their few remaining ancient trees, the great bodies of water that provide for magnificent whales, the air we breathe—all are withering rapidly, much too rapidly.

It is said that challenges provide opportunity. The good news is that, at consciousness' leading edge, we understand the need for alignment and have already developed all the solutions that are required to live in harmony with other people and with Nature. The worsening degradation is the very thing that is catalyzing our new understandings, thereby starting the healing process.

Our current human epoch's moral and spiritual challenge is the ecological crisis. Our generation's solutions or, alternatively, failure to act will define the legacy we leave our children and all those who follow. This situation is nothing less than the catalyst for the next step in the evolution of our species, that is, our advancing human consciousness. Within this context the story addresses the challenges incumbent on our human circumstances and our vulnerability to potential chaos and disaster. Examining life through this creation story helps us to understand our predicament and provides solutions to the hurdles we face.

Will we continue to desecrate the Earth, its people, and its remarkable creatures, or will we change course and transform ourselves into a peaceful, life-affirming, relational society based upon newly revealed, expanded consciousness? Relationships and intimacies are key: parent to child, person to person, culture to differing culture, religion to religion, and especially *Homo sapiens* to the natural world.

Most people have more than enough to worry about just going to work, paying the bills, and dealing with family problems. It's asking a lot of the typical person on the street to take responsibility for the looming environmental crisis in addition to modern life's many demands; however, there are many reasons for doing so, reasons that are both altruistic and self-serving. The story presented in the following pages shows us why "mutually beneficial reciprocity" is the most meaningful way to live our lives. Each person can add meaning to his or her life, including profound depth and joy, by participating in today's advancing human consciousness. In this story we learn how to become more intimate with our world and thereby to change our outlook and our actions, eventually resulting in healthier and more sustainable lifestyles for each of us and for the planet.

So far, we lack the courage to implement this newfound wisdom; however, integrating this new understanding, which I'm calling Ecological Epoch consciousness, is essential if we are to avoid chaos and devastation. If successful, we will have saved our children from the inexpressible horror of living through the shriveling and decimation of Earth's ecosystems. At the same time, we will have engaged in a more meaningful and joyous lifetime.

The books are a call to a deeper awareness and to progressive social change and involvement. They encourage conscious activism. This twofold engagement in the world provides a more profound view of reality. It also reveals the skillful means to liberate a compassionate heart—our own and that of others. We will show how to follow Nature's lead and organically grow an Earth community that has concern for people from all nations, all religions, and all races.

The world is different from our current perception of it. By changing the way we *see* the world to a worldview that is more in alignment with the way Nature functions—with actual reality—we will change our methods of relating to each other, the Earth, and all living things. The next step in the evolution of human consciousness has recently occurred, but we have not integrated this newfound wisdom into our personal and social behaviors. Change we must, and change we shall; whether by inspiration or by catastrophic pain, the final result will be the same. It is inevitable that, whether ten billion or two billion humans remain fifty years from now, our species as a whole shall eventually move into the Ecological Epoch.

Our Human Story: An Overview

As we awaken to a new understanding of the human condition, we find ourselves in an odd predicament. The Earth is withering. For the first time ever, our world is diminishing. When Homo sapiens first walked the Earth about two hundred thousand years ago, we were enmeshed in the sacred life matrix; this is called Natural Harmony in our story. We developed more sophisticated logical thought; we learned from Nature and from trial and error; for many millennia, our actions were compatible with our surroundings; we became clever, yet our lives remained immersed in Earth's mystical surrounds; more time passed, and new human capabilities emerged as our reflective consciousness uncovered amazing new interconnections—discoveries that changed human life.

We became fully modern humans (Homo sapiens) about two hundred thousand years ago. This was a time when everything was wild; as nothing had been "tamed," there was no conceptual ability to distinguish tame from wild. Like all other species, we were fully embedded in the wild. Our brains were full-sized and capable of learning all that we now know; however, it took incalculable trial and error sessions combined with our big-brained ingenuity to build the knowledge we now command. Intuition guided the way; we were finely attuned to the senses and emotions, allowing deep immersion in the natural world. An ever-alert concern for survival meant that respect and appreciation for our surroundings was a necessary priority. Paying attention to Nature's intricacies was essential. This is how our early modern ancestors honed their intelligence: which plants are edible, which are medicinal, which are toxic? Which animals can be successfully hunted? Which hunting techniques will be successful with which animal? These were survival questions that required total focus.

Detailed observation of plant characteristics and animal habits sharpened our early skill sets and knitted our neuron pathways. Total immersion in Natural Harmony contributed to our species' early success. Logical thinking played a role by facilitating language skills, inventive tool use, and hunting strategies. A rational mind was needed to build an immense knowledge library that was then taught to the next generation. Human language skills became more sophisticated, facilitating faster learning through enhanced communication. All this occurred within the milieu of Natural Harmony. Intuition led the way, supported by logic.

Humans immigrated out of Africa in waves, populating the Middle East, Asia, and Europe. Manufactured stone tools became more sophisticated. Changes began to appear; the planet's megafauna began to decline and eventually disappear. Our fellow large-brained Homo sapiens, the Neanderthals, disappeared, after sharing territory for many thousands of years with humans whom had migrated into their territory from Africa. Two human "wisdom-reservoirs," collective intuition and *collective logic, now became more explicitly engaged with each other, vying for influence within human societies; their respective cultural influences would ebb and flow, wrestling with one another for prominence throughout the ensuing eras.*

We began our modern human period immersed in the wild and in the sacred Earth; we settled in towns and cities, becoming "tame" ourselves and gradually losing immersion in, and gratitude for, wild Nature. For a few millennia, there was a balance between the tame and the wild, between fear of Nature and respect for Nature. Time passed; cultures changed. Removed from Nature, living in cities with large populations to feed, seasonal vicissitudes and potential crop failures elicited scarcity fears, demanding animal and even human sacrifice—nudging societies toward vengeful gods. Eventually our reasoning powers came to dominate; our previously balanced relationship with sacred Nature began to tilt asunder. Science was born in this cultural milieu; it attempted to subdue Nature, prodding her inner sanctity to extract secrets that, eventually, would unwittingly be used to abuse her integrity. The damage this caused has catalyzed a transformation of consciousness into the Ecological Epoch.

This human-centric overview outlines our evolving enterprise on Planet Earth; however, our creation story goes back much further to the beginning of time, 13.8 billion years ago. *Book One: In the Beginning* is a scientific-mythological story about how we came to be human.

CHAPTER 1

CHANGING OUR WORLDVIEW CHANGES THE WORLD

You must understand the whole of life, not just one little part of it. That is why you must read. That is why you must look at the skies, that is why you must sing and dance, and write poems and suffer and understand, for all that is life.

—J. Krishnamurti

Sophia's Revelations: Introductory Story

I have explored many religious and alternative spiritual traditions over a thirty-five-year period. This off-and-on immersion has included time with many "old masters," including the Dalai Lama, J. Krishnamurti,

Muktananda, and Thich Nhat Hanh, among others. For example, years ago, I completed a five-day meditation on Whidbey Island in Washington State; a small, twelve-person group sat in a cathedral-ceilinged, glass-walled room next to a meadow. To get to this lush, garden-like field, we traversed a narrow wooden walkway above a small wetland within an exotic temperate rainforest. The walk was like passing through a portal from the mundane to the magical. After meditating for several days, my dreams changed; I began to "wake up" within my dream—an altered state called "lucid dreaming" that I have experienced off and on throughout my life.

While in this lucid state, I was visited by Sophia, an ethereal-looking woman who appeared to be in her mid-forties. She was dressed in a multipleated, pure white diaphanous robe. A greenish hue surrounded her, which I took to be an energetic aura. I asked, "Who are you?" She smiled graciously but did not answer that question; however, she did offer to address my numerous "existential concerns." Over several dream sessions during the next few nights, we had many long discussions. Although I took notes as soon as I awoke, there was much more information imparted than I was able to remember and record.

The first time she appeared, I asked why the world's religions were so dysfunctional that they were literally at war with each other. Her response:

Unbeknownst to fundamentalists in all religions, spirituality has no "right" or "wrong" to it. Naturally, there is a huge range of ideas, practices, and dogma connected to the world's many spiritual traditions. At their core they all connect to the one spiritual essence; however, their followers become confused into thinking that theirs is the only pathway to divine connection. In actuality, there are infinite avenues that arrive at the same end point. Here are several ways to discern a sacred spiritual practice: whether or not it helps its adherents to feel closer to the Divine; whether it imbues their lives with grace, love, and meaning; whether they feel connected to a larger community of people in empathetic, constructive ways; whether they recognize their kinship with Earth's entire 'community of all beings.

The following day, I wandered in the meditation meadow, crossing the grassy, flower-laden field without paying much attention to the physical world. My eyes were half focused; I had only partial awareness of the puffy green carpet beneath my bare feet, protruding between my toes, step by step. When I stopped near a large, hanging branch, my attention was drawn upward. To my delighted surprise, I discovered that I had almost bumped into a massive, ancient cedar tree. I gazed up at the cedar looking down at me from its seventy-foot height. Perhaps this is how a mother's body appears to a newborn staring upward.

During that night's lucid dream, I stood near the same giant tree, with Sophia nearby. She said, *"So, Mr. Cedar, what can you say to us?"* A tree-voice came from within the dense structure: *"We Nature Beings have given the humans our trust; they have yet to fulfill their potential and, as such, have become dangerous—the damage is extensive. When the people hurt us and destroy us, they have violated our trust; they have betrayed us and thereby diminished themselves."*

In the depth of the following four nights, I had various questions answered. The responses that I was able to corral from these revelations are presented below.

I asked Sophia how to describe "spirit." Her response:

Spirit is a primordial essence emanating from the Creative Source that infuses all life (including life force to be found in minerals, metals, rocks, ocean waters, and other inanimate 'things'). Spirit is an essence that connects us to the Divine and is an indefinable aspect of the Creative Source. Spirit imbues each body with life force.

There is an ethereal bond connecting all matter in the Universe; in ancient Greek mythology, it was called Eros and was the first 'thing' manifested from Chaos when the Universe was born. When embodied, Eros is experienced as love and beauty.

Recognition that all matter is sacred and is woven together in Natural Harmony provides a connection to the universal spirit-essence and a better comprehension of the divine Creative Source, which can be experienced but not logically described.

There is no human scientific understanding, as yet, for the physical mechanism at play in the energetic fields comprising spirit, but soon humans will better understand the physical interaction connecting all matter at the subatomic level. This will help them to see how spirit imbues and influences the material world.

As human consciousness deepens, it expands one's body as a spirit vessel; there is an ebb and flow to this system. A person's spirit is enhanced commensurate with her appreciation and gratitude for the gift of life, which brings more intimacy, meaning, and joy. Deepening awareness provides spaciousness for spirit. The more advanced one's stage of consciousness, the more internal spaciousness is provided for spirit to flow into one's body and reside there. When spirit is depleted, it will part ways with the body, resulting in physical death.

During the following midnight liaison, I questioned Sophia about "God." We discussed whether or not God and "evil" are related. She told me:

There is no rational description, no conceptual approach that can encompass the Creative Source; all attempts are futile, misleading, confusing, and counterproductive. Connection to Creative Source can be accessed through feelings and intuition. One is most open to the divine experience while residing in the present moment without judgments and opinions; this is a process called "letting be" so that we may be empty to receive the Divine.

The term evil represents an artificial human construct— a mind-created idea—that is conceived in an attempt to cope with various existential fears. What we call "evil" could more appropriately be referred to as "disharmony that causes disruption and, at times, destruction." Fear, chaos, and destruction are real; evil does not exist.

Our discussion was much more detailed; I remember only the high-lights. Time stood still, but the enchanted encounter continued. I asked my new wisdom-bearer to describe the connections and relationships that Native Americans refer to as the "web of life." She responded:

All manifest things are sacred matter, organized as Natural Harmony, the mutually beneficial reciprocity woven into life's matrix. The relationships contained within Natural Harmony are a window to the Divine.

There is a critically important connection among individuals, the entire human population, and all other species. A person with this consciousness is normally compassionate and empathetic and consequently does not engage in gratuitous destruction—not even for the seduction of financial profit or 'making a living' to feed his or her family. The 'world family,' human and nonhuman, becomes adopted into this person's own family.

All things, all beings emanate from 'Oneness,' an undifferentiated essence in which subject and object have no meaning. The physical world manifests in sacred wholeness, a gestalt of unique things in which everything relates to every other thing; this is called Natural Harmony.

Appreciation for Nature's wonders is directly proportional to Divine connection. Recognition and knowledge of Natural Harmony is related to expanded human consciousness; these understandings are proportional to one's compassion, empathy, love, and ability to celebrate life.

The following night I again awoke to meet this timeless mentor—perhaps a ghost and goddess combined—who was helping me to structure life's most profound mysteries into a comprehendible poetic collage. I asked her to tell me how to live in the "sacred," day to day. She replied:

There are many valid spiritual paths and practices; all such practices lead to a deeper understanding of the nature of reality and to the same transpersonal revelations. To live in gratitude is to fully accept the gift of life, thereby experiencing heaven on Earth. Acceptance, trust, and forgiveness are qualities that accompany appreciation and gratitude. 'Letting be' is an element of being in the moment.

Babies come into the world with expanded consciousness and full-blown ties to their spiritual origin; however, they are soon acculturated with information, some valid, some mistaken and confusing; this information-instilling process contracts consciousness. Personal growth requires pushing through the influence of this acculturation, recognizing the difference between valid and invalid information, thereby deepening one's conscious understanding of reality. Honest spiritual practices aid this endeavor.

One's personal meaning and joy are directly proportional to one's consciousness, which can be advanced through focused practice; levels and stages of human consciousness enhance one's incarnate spirit. Levels advance within stages; stages advance as cultures deepen and become more complex. The higher the stage and the level within the stage, the more divine interaction one will experience."

In our final session, corresponding to the last meditation practice, she once more appeared but this time began to talk without my questioning her:

> *The more one invites and embodies spirit, the closer one's connection to divine presence—the Creative Source. Day-to-day suffering can be relieved through meditation and other 'liberation pathways'; further liberation from self-absorption can be achieved through introspection. Appreciation and gratitude allow us to celebrate life and live in Natural Harmony.*
>
> *When one appreciates beauty and feels love, he or she is experiencing Natural Harmony. This proximity imbues one's life with meaning and joy in addition to spaciousness for spirit-presence and awareness. Eros provides an ethereal connection among all things. When finally immersed in this consciousness, people will enhance the world. Rampant destruction will end.*
>
> *I am available to you at any time, as long as you come to me with humility and respect for all creation; I speak for all things, large and small. Come to me with an honest desire to know the world's sacred nature. Come to me within special circumstances and with pure intention. I am Eros, the love that joins all things in innumerable exotic life-dances.*

With these statements, our dream session ended. I awoke to a world that had not changed but, to me, had more depth and meaning. The meditation retreat had ended.

I have called upon Sophia for the past twenty-five years. Most often she appears while I am away from my normal routine, sometimes while traveling to remote or exotic places. The personal stories distributed throughout this book recount various encounters with this wisdom guide. In many respects Sophia's "revelations" have inspired the research that eventually became this New Creation Story. I wanted to know if I could validate these insights using scientific, philosophic, and spiritual information readily available in contemporary literature.

As I pursued this endeavor, month after month, there was a resonance between these revelations and what I discovered during my research that made this two-year writing project worthwhile. In some respects this entire book is an investigation of Sophia's comments, presented in the preceding pages. I make no judgment about their validity or about whether or not they were a transmission from a "transpersonal" source or not. Perhaps they are entirely from my own intuition. But is one's intuition personal or transpersonal?

To love is to be in communion with the other and to discover in that other the spark of God.

— Paulo Coelho

Navigating Today's Dangerous Waters

Many of us recognize that we are at a critical juncture in our species' evolution. As discussed in my prior book, *Consciousness in Action*, during the past 120 years of "industrial revolution," a new planetary danger has arisen: the Earth bleeds on the cross of human industry. Our unsustainable economic system is a voracious engine that consumes more than the Earth can restore. Its community of life has been created from interconnections that are bound together as delicate fibers, both physical and ethereal; once lost, it's unlikely they can be restored.

We are facing ecological, economic, and social collapses that affect every aspect of our lives as well as the future of humanity and the living Earth. Much of what no longer works in our world originates from an outdated worldview, that is, scientific materialism. It is an old story that sees the Universe as dead matter and the Earth as boundlessly exploitable. What is the new story? Is it capable of guiding us past our dangerously contracted cultural understanding of reality to make Earth a healthy place for our children?

Many are asking questions: What can I do? Do my actions really matter? Where might I intervene and attempt to create positive change? The New Creation Story presented in the following pages examines where we humans have come from and where we are going. It describes how we have begun a transformation that imbues life with more meaning. Effort, luck, and a spiritual outlook can perhaps integrate this new human consciousness, the latest stage in human evolution, into our social behavior.

A successful navigation of today's planetwide dangers requires a bridging from our current "outlook" to a worldview that embodies a deepened understanding of the nature of reality. Changing our minds can change the world. Our human worldview has always been evolving. Although still in its infancy, it is evolving now! We have awakened the next step in human evolution. This story shows us how to restore our planet by creating a healthier culture—perhaps a *Tao Te Ching* for contemporary times, a guide attuning us to Nature's flow, showing us the mutually beneficial reciprocity woven into life's matrix. This interweaving and intimacy has allowed life on Earth to endure and evolve for more than three billion years.

For those of us who live in wealthy societies, our inventive ingenuity, based on scientific materialism, dominates our collective worldview. It is primarily manifested as consumerism: produce more, consume more, accumulate more; this has become the most prominent mind-set of our contemporary culture. It frequently creates a sense of isolation and meaninglessness in our lives.

We have become desensitized, numb to the ongoing planetwide despoliation because we are disconnected from Nature's beauty and depth; consequently, we are willing to damage our environment so drastically that we endanger its health and our very survival. *Our collective internal turmoil becomes reflected in our external world, and our dysfunction is projected out into the world*, resulting in the extinction of species, devastating climate change, and nuclear meltdowns.

Our attitude toward the world is shaping the physical and biological character of our planet. Our manner of "seeing" is, to a large extent, a cultural bias. The stories we tell each other about our origins, our creation stories, inform our culture and affect our behavior. Scientific materialism dominates our worldview; it is literally creating the Earth's future. Our level of appreciation or disdain for the Earth's healthy functioning will determine our sacred planet's health—or its continued withering.

Especially in the past sixty-five years, since about 1945, we have been moving in a negative direction. Respect, gratitude, and reverence have, for the most part, been discarded from our cultural priorities.

These pages address the potential outcomes, from positive to disastrous, of our human-centered (anthropocentric) arrogance. What is the prognosis? We humans are just as natural as flowers and other creatures, a rapidly evolving and unfinished experiment of the living, dynamic Earth. If we become too burdensome on the Earth's ecosystems, the planet is quite capable of "sloughing us off" for the health of the whole. What means of salvation will direct us toward healthy interactions with the Earth and promote its vitality? This is the conundrum we address.

The damage we are causing is the impetus driving our evolutionary change. It is evidence of birth pains associated with the delivery of the next generation of consciousness—one that will replace this production-consumption era. This book is a new story, reviewing where we humans originated and describing the species we are becoming. These changes are occurring now—a rebirthing process; however, there is no way to know if it can stem the destructive tide of corporate and political greed in time to avoid social and biological chaos. Which will be the legacy we leave to our children?

Our creation story includes setbacks:

When the human population becomes unmanageable; when corporate agriculture forces rural populations into the cities to find work; when cities need more and more water, causing lakes to dry up; the wetlands retreat, the fish die; the Great

Heron flies away; the trees wilt, the shade is diminished, the rain is reduced; the lush grasses fail; the deer have no food and leave the area; the coyotes and mountain lions have nothing to eat; then, finally, the dry lakebed becomes a dust bowl, blowing in the wind.

...and shows us a way forward:

Natural Harmony pervades the Universe and is the relational fabric that binds all life on Earth together; its core characteristic is "mutually beneficial reciprocity" that allows life to endure and evolve over vast time frames. It is the container for life's biological propensity to become more and more complex as our planet ages. All mountains, all rivers, all oceans, all air, all breath, all plants, all animals—all things are joined in Natural Harmony. Human consciousness has constantly evolved and is currently continuing its evolutionary process at a faster and faster pace. Its deepening connection to Natural Harmony is a movement toward the Creative Source—the unexplainable energy behind the Big Bang that created our cosmos.

The way we see ourselves in relation to other life-forms and to the Earth's living systems will largely define our success or failure as a species. We are just now, after seven million years of biological evolution, after discovering so many secrets of the Earth's inner workings, coming to a crossroads unlike any other. Recently our anthropomorphic egocentrism, outdated religions, and ingenuity have confused us into misinterpreting our appropriate place in Earth's animal community. Our economies are destroying the habitat for most other large animals and for ourselves.

Because we misunderstand our place in life's larger gestalt, our worldview, our attitude, and our behavior are literally creating our planet's physical constitution—the reality we are leaving for our children. Our production-consumption social priority is not organic. It is an artificial aberration; as such, its existence is delicate, and its temporary benefits are near collapse. The decline has begun, and as a result, the destruction we are causing is forcing us to take the next step in the evolution of human consciousness: a deepened understanding of humanity's healthy interaction with the remaining natural world.

There are now two fields of consciousness competing for the human soul. We are currently pursuing a course that has the potential to create incomprehensible suffering for our children's children in the process of destroying the majority of life-forms that exist on the planet today; at the same time, we are tapping into a more profound reality. We perceive the many threads needed to weave a new fabric within the human psyche; we are beginning to create healthier connections among ourselves and other species and to have new respect for the Earth's living systems.

Our quest draws us ever closer to the sanctity of the Creative Source and to life's sacred nature. If we fail, we fail. The Earth will survive and produce more of her incredible life-forms. Perhaps a new species will come forward in another seven million years to advance biological consciousness further than we were able to. The jury is out as to which energetic flow will prevail: will it be giant corporations consuming the Earth or, conversely, empowered individuals sharing newly discovered, life-affirming information by social media? Because either outcome could occur, it is most important that as many concerned people as possible participate in finding solutions and demanding public policy changes. Only a massive intervention will prevent chaos over the next thirty to fifty years. Outrage and protest is required; visionary solutions to create alternative energy and sustainable economies are essential, as is charitable service to feed the children, restore denuded mountains, and clean polluted oceans.

It is not necessary to reach consensus or even a majority. When a critical mass of caring world citizens comes together, a new energy field will surround the globe, lighting up this new consciousness and spreading it to the remaining people. Those at the leading edge of this movement have been given the wisdom to direct the process. Platforms are needed so their voices can be heard.

Natural Harmony provides an ethical guide for all human behavior, both individual and social. Each decision point can be weighed for its benefits to the Earth community and against its potential negative effects. In times gone by many indigenous groups made decisions based on the impacts affecting future generations, anticipating several hundred years into the future. There are many techniques that an individual can use to connect to Natural Harmony; these "practices" are liberating. They result in expanded awareness and less egocentrism, hence their increased popularity in recent years. Walking or sitting quietly in Nature; silent prayer; meditation; yoga; sacred dance; chanting; spiritual music; art; and even long-distance running, which floods one's body with endorphins and flushes away stale emotions, are some examples.

The Ecological Epoch reveals the continuing evolutionary movement toward enlightenment—knowledge of the sacred Creative Source. Its core qualities are connection and intimacy. Taking part in this new development is not onerous; quite the contrary, it is the most meaningful, fulfilling, and joyous life one could have. It's good for the soul; it brings us into contact with other loving, creative people; it serves our children and life itself; and it brings us closer to God, the Great Sprit, and the Tao.

It is likely that our ancestors' mental acuity was formed, over eons of time, by discovering intimate associations. They were focused on the "hunt" to provide food and to notice the subtle qualities that distinguish edible or medicinal plants from their toxic cousins. In later epochs human intellectual focus was needed to develop agriculture and to learn to live together in large villages. Later still, we refined symbolic thought and developed written language; then, scientific knowledge created industrial-scale invention, causing both construction and destruction.

Times have changed; each human era has had its primary challenges. There is now a new mental, emotional, and spiritual task looming. *Our current evolutionary awakenings are coming from new insights about our interrelatedness with the Earth's dynamic systems.* In each advancing evolutionary stage of consciousness, it is the pressure of our human-to-Nature healthy functioning that catalyzes deepened awareness. We are on the cusp of a new era, born of our excesses. Thus, you and I are thrust into the crisis, and opportunity, of this human epoch. Deepened human consciousness is the driving force behind cultural change and social behavior. Solving traumatic existential challenges requires new ways of seeing the world, that is, an awakening of new human consciousness.

Defining Consciousness

What is consciousness? In its simplest form the term *consciousness* can be defined as awareness of one's objective and subjective "life-framework" at any particular moment. During normal waking hours, as each moment unfolds, an individual entertains various thoughts. There are exceptions to this rule: sometimes, strong sensations take precedence, for example, during sexual orgasm, or the occurrence of a physical injury, or at the onset of a new love; during meditation one is perhaps able to become "thoughtless," but all these are special "altered-state" circumstances.

Our moment-to-moment consciousness is typically contained by the immediate set of thoughts in our awareness. Do animals have conscious awareness? Of course they do. Is it the same as human awareness? No, consciousness differs from species to species; similarly, there is a wide range within each species. Studying human consciousness makes this variety abundantly obvious. For the most part human adults "think" in worded concepts based on their primary language, but not exclusively.

Some people are able to "think" in images; perhaps the uncanny success of early Egyptian art, architecture, hieroglyphs, and much more was made possible by this "thinking" mode. Some individuals with a mental disorder called "savant syndrome" have special consciousness abilities unavailable to most people, made possible from their different perceptual functioning; they often exhibit exceptional talent in art, music, memory, or rapid calculation. Accomplished scientists often think and even dream in the scientific "language" of equations. Large-brained mammals, including elephants, whales, and some nonhuman primates, may be as intelligent as humans; however, their modes of perception differ dramatically. The term *consciousness* encompasses all these types of awareness and much more.

One who appreciates art or music is able to be "fully conscious of" a beautiful sunset or an exciting musical composition, purposely setting aside his or her "thoughts." Composing music can occur without thinking, and some compositions "appear" to the musician fully formed. Orchestrations sometimes "come to" a musician while he or she is asleep, dreaming. I have had this experience myself.

There is interplay between subjective consciousness and objective consciousness constantly occurring during waking hours—an interactive give-and-take between one's interior thoughts and sensations vis-à-vis one's mental and physical interaction with the exterior world of "things."

Both awareness types exist simultaneously, competing for conscious attention. Sometimes multiple awarenesses are possible, that is, holding several forms of consciousness concurrently; some individuals are better at this "multitasking" than others.

All this and more could be referred to as "consciousness." For our purposes, let's refine the definition to make it more specific to this book's objectives. In these pages, unless otherwise indicated, when referring to embodied consciousness the term will mean self-reflective human consciousness, that is, the ability to, and the process of, being aware of one's consciousness. One example is thinking about thinking—philosophy often falls into this category—or thinking about interior sensations, or analyzing a musical composition.

Mountain gorillas are meticulously aware of their surroundings; in this respect they are conscious. Whales make music, but there's no evidence as to whether or not they "think about" that music. Elephants "think" in ways that are mysterious and intriguing to us humans; they mourn their dead, sometime returning to their loved ones' places of death. They can paint scenes by holding a paintbrush with their trunks; however, there is no evidence that they are "thinking about" those depictions. Perhaps the earliest known human pictographs from about ninety thousand years ago were rendered with a similar consciousness.

Biological evolution creates vessels for consciousness to evolve; the whale has a very high intelligence, perhaps with more potential than human intelligence. Environmental circumstances were different for the whale during its fifty-million-year evolutionary development. It's possible that there has not yet been enough environmental challenge for a whale's reflective consciousness to evolve (most whale species had no predators until humans began hunting them).

It's also possible that whales, elephants, and some other large-brained mammals have already surpassed our intelligence with different forms of consciousness—dimensions that we cannot measure because we are ignorant of them—such as sacred Earth-consciousness. For example, elephants are typically nonaggressive and vegetarian; they have few enemies. Perhaps, similar to the whales' history, these survival circumstances were not challenging enough to require reflective consciousness; however, elephants may have developed more deeply felt compassion and intuition than we humans.

Consciousness has a propensity to express itself biologically—and not just in *H. sapiens*. This was true for the Neanderthals, who some anthropologists theorize were more intuitive, less logical thinking than our foreparents; therefore, they were less skilled at planning and scheming. This may have led to their demise at the hands of *H. sapiens*, although interbreeding also occurred. The point is that consciousness, including reflective consciousness that is currently the exclusive domain of humans, will continue to press for expression in multiple species as future millennia unfold.

In any case, self-reflective consciousness will be our bellwether for these pages—the capacity to think about thinking. This concept was introduced to English writing in the seventeenth century with the translation of, and reference to, the Latin term, *conscius sibi*, meaning "knowing with one's own self," which is a way of saying that one is interacting with or contemplating one's own knowledge. This early use in the Latin language dates back to the Roman Empire. The concept's roots came to the

Romans from classical Greek philosophy, indicating that the discussion of self-reflective consciousness has been around for at least a few thousand years.

> *Recognizing our sacred place within the community of all life and behaving likewise is a spiritual calling.*

Two Rivers

What are the ways in which we may accelerate our evolution, before massive-scale ecological or social catastrophe occurs? Our contemporary culture is a confluence of two rivers of energy. One features the scientific-production-consumption worldview of the past several hundred years. The other is an emergent stage of consciousness in which the living planet, Gaia, is the center of attention. Will we destabilize the weather patterns to the extent that coastal zones permanently flood, food production areas are left in drought, clean drinking water is hard to find, and the resulting "economic refugees" pour out into the few remaining viable human habitats, creating irreconcilable social unrest everywhere? Or will we deepen our understanding of the web of life and act on what we learn?

I propose that the planet's health and our species' future depend on a series of individual and society-wide awakenings based on a more profound understanding of life itself. This information emerges from our New Creation Story—one that only our current epoch can birth. The story redefines our purpose as individuals and as a species. The old stories do not adequately address our current existential challenges.

A new story is needed to guide our society, indeed our entire species, through the shallow water in which we're floundering: climate change, careless genetic engineering, nuclear waste toxicity, and much more. These things were not in our awareness, so they did not appear in earlier creation stories that discussed man's fall from paradise, angry gods, dominion over the beasts and superiority above other animals, and so on. We created the pretense that we are not animals. Our stories invented an anthropocentric viewpoint, claiming superiority for humans. Our New Story is different, emphasizing relatedness, not domination.

In an earlier book, I use the term *liberation pathways* to describe the many processes that can expand our awareness, heal our wounds, reduce our fears, and thereby ally us with Nature. Is there time to complete this process? I don't know the answer—none of us does—but that's what makes participation in the adventure even more compelling. Everyone can help—each person has a unique ability to "see" differently, to listen deeply and find solutions; each has a special circumstance and life experience. Seeing our human story with new eyes can provide insight into the planet's health, personal-spiritual meaning, and fairness in society—all so that we can function more successfully, living together on our beautiful planet.

To live in appreciation is the most fulfilling way to live one's life—to be fully alive. This is a "waking up" that provides well-being in contrast to the consternation inherent in our society's production-consumption ethic and the consequent stress that we deal with our entire lives.

Will we succeed in turning things around in time? I am "hopeful," but that's not the same as "optimistic." We're in a real mess, which has become the challenge of our current human epoch. Our ancestors had different challenges. Ours require our newly changed consciousness to be rapidly integrated into our economic policies and our treatment of Nature. Participating in this adventure is the most exciting way to spend one's life. The thirteenth-century Zen philosopher Dōgen said, "Enlightenment is intimacy with all things." A corollary is that the more we are able to deeply connect to any particular thing, the more profound our life experience becomes.

Species extinctions, chemical toxicity and atmospheric pollution assault both Nature and human well-being. How should we proceed? Will this immensity promote personal paralysis or stimulate change? Without a rapid change in our attitude, that is, without our adopting an ecological consciousness, the world as we know it will be lost. Our blessing is that all the pieces are in place, the wisdom is at hand to turn around and to appreciate life. Living in intimacy is mutually beneficial for all things. Participation in this process adds meaning and beauty to one's life. *This Creation Story is about intimacy, creating community, and finding joy—all through interrelationship.* In taking the next courageous steps, we are creating a new human species and celebrating our unique capacity for self-reflection, for honoring beauty, and for living in love.

But the Jewish tradition also contains...a sort of intoxicated joy and amazement at the beauty and grandeur of this world, of which man can form just a faint notion. This joy is the feeling from which true scientific research draws its spiritual sustenance, but which also seems to find expression in the song of birds.

—Albert Einstein, 1934

CHAPTER 2

THE GRAND PERSPECTIVE: WHO AM I, AND WHAT AM I DOING HERE?

It's about sixty years ago, 1952. I am living in Clearwater, Florida, a town of ten thousand people, mostly built up over the prior eighty years beside a tranquil bay formed from a narrow barrier-island sand spit on the Gulf of Mexico. My name is Andrew, and I am a Caucasian of Scottish decent. I'm seven years old. The world's population is about 2.6 billion. Looking at a paper-flat 2-D world map, I find it curious that the western shape of Africa and the eastern shape of South America look like puzzle-pieces that would fit together perfectly, but my early fifties-era schoolteacher does not yet know that the Earth's thin crust drifts atop the magna as "continental shelves."

In Sunday school I learn about heaven and hell; we sing about angels at Christmastime. My stepmother invites a young minister to our home some afternoons to personally explain the rewards of behaving properly, especially the necessity to do what my parents tell me to do, so that I will not burn in hell. Something seems "fishy" about the whole story; I'm not convinced that this information is valid.

The explanations don't add up for me, but the unspoken beauty of the surrounding wetlands does have meaning. Strange, neither my teachers nor my ministers mention the birds, the wetlands, or the vast warm-water gulf that surrounds us, defining our town. Last summer my family rented a beach house for a few weeks. The morning after arriving, I was the first one up, drawn outside by a glorious sunrise on the water. I went out alone into Nature for the first time in my short life, a solitary, silent seven-year-old boy wandering the lively water's edge at sunrise. Seabirds everywhere were squawking in call and response, creating a glorious cacophony of early morning feeding.

This is my church—one without words. The rest seems muddled, the wordy teachings confused. My human-oriented world offers physical safety but no love. There is little meaning or purpose in my life other than the deeply satisfying connection to the birds and beach, a sacred communion that I keep to myself. Parents, teachers, preachers, and other adults don't really have any interesting stuff to say. I'm not alone per se, but I am lonely.

Human consciousness is changing rapidly. These pages examine the crisis and opportunity of our current human epoch, which has become the Ecological Epoch. The story provides an overview of our predicament while examining ways to successfully meet the challenges we face. We examine "deep time" and the human condition: where we came from, who we are as a species, and why we are capable of solving the most serious challenges that our planet's creatures have faced over the past sixty-five million years. This new look at human beings is framed as a creation story, utilizing science, anthropology, human origins, philosophy, spirituality, and our intimate association with the natural world.

Who are we as a species? How might we more effectively address our planetwide challenges by understanding our origins differently? Today's current cultural story is primarily science based: cosmology, life origins, paleontology, biology, geology, biochemistry, archeology, anthropology, early civilizations, Cartesian science, philosophy, psychology, traditional religion—all of which are assertive and, to some extent, masculine in form and presentation. Our new story incorporates all this earlier wisdom and ads new insights, which are expressed within an intuitive, spiritual context. It is based on consciousness in general, human consciousness in particular, and the evolution of all consciousness, which necessarily includes art, music, dance, athletic movement, spiritual practice, mythology, mystical religion, metaphysics, Eros, and other arenas that are primarily in the realm of intuition and body wisdom, representing "feminine" values. Surprisingly, today's "new science" also validates a more relational worldview.

Our creation story is the interplay—a dance between the two: it is the Divine Feminine coming to know the Enlightened Masculine for the first time. The Divine Feminine has been with us a long time, emerging in the Upper Paleolithic and early Neolithic in conjunction with advancing spirituality. Approximately five thousand years ago, this Divine Feminine influence in human affairs was subjugated by the "adolescent masculine," characterized by dominating enthusiasm and exuberant strength. Now, the Enlightened Masculine has made its appearance on the human consciousness stage in today's emerging Ecological Epoch. This new consciousness is now dancing with the Divine Feminine. Both are needed to solve our current ecological crisis.

We are immersed in an interactive and interrelational universal whole. Most importantly, we belong to a complex biological Earth community. In what respects are we out of alignment with our own biosphere, and how did this condition come about? To answer these questions, our story weaves multiple threads into a fabric that reveals more human consciousness. Like most creation stories, this one is spiritually based and accessed primarily through mystical experience. Each section is a puzzle piece belonging to the big picture, which is our creation story.

We are built from atoms that were created by intense heat and pressure inside stars; these particles exploded out into space, eventually coalescing. Stardust and star gas formed our planet, Earth; carbon atoms interacted with other elements and came to life; divine complexity built even more mysterious life-forms; bacteria combined to form sophisticated cells which, in turn, grew into large plants and animals. From a broad perspective, carbon molecules built dinosaurs. Time passed. Conditions changed. Most very large life-forms died away.

Later, mammals grew bigger, and some returned to the sea to become whales. Primates appeared and evolved into human beings. Carbon-based Homo sapiens networked neuron cells into incredible intelligence. As intelligence grew in plant cells and animal brains, mysterious interconnections were revealed to human beings. Science ruled the day; incredible inventions appeared.

Consumer goods, income, and production and distribution of these "goods" soon became the basis for social ethics. The physical planet began to wither. Not yet fully understood, disembodied collective intelligence (called "logosphere" and "intuosphere" in our story) came to life. Human consciousness deepened. Artificial intelligence emerged, creating cyberspace. The mentality of destruction from the scientific period began to be met head-on and heart-on in the newly emerging Ecological Epoch.

Disruptions from the Fossil-Fuel Epoch

Our story's ending is as yet unknown but will be revealed during the coming decades. There are numerous current challenges, both social and environmental, that we will address in these pages as we redefine our kinship to the natural world and explore our reintegration. However, the big issue, the proverbial "elephant in the room," is climate change. The doubling of Earth's population in my lifetime; the current unsustainable world economic model; the pollution of land, sea, and air; the loss of biodiversity—all these issues and many more have to be addressed; however, climate change is currently the dagger that presses against our jugular vein.

The Holocene epoch is a geologic period that began about twelve thousand years ago at the end of the Pleistocene. The Holocene's warming weather allowed human agriculture to take hold about eleven thousand years ago. This corresponded to the Neolithic Period (meaning "New Stone Age," referring to human technology and advances in stone tool design and effectiveness), which began about 10,400 years ago. The Holocene has been a period of stability: climatic, geologic, atmospheric, biologic, hydrologic, and oceanic. Prior to this time, humans lived through extreme variations in climatic conditions, cycles of warming and cooling that created a series of ice ages and other harsh challenges.

So why is it different now? Why can we not "suck it up" (as my football coaches used to say) and deal with the coming discomforts? Answers are clear: prior to the Holocene epoch, we were all hunter-gatherers, living in roving bands, following the seasons, the fruits, and the prey—our food. It is unlikely that human population exceeded 100 million, which is about 1.5 percent of today's seven billion plus. In addition, we moderns have established our cities next to the oceans and rivers, expanding these cities' population manifold over several thousand years, with confidence that sea levels would remain stable; rivers would continue to provide clean, abundant water; and rainfall would nurture our plantings in the planet's limited fertile soils. For the first time since our ancestors settled the Fertile Crescent ten thousand years ago, climate stability has ended; our confidence is now misplaced. We face the prospect of hundreds of millions, perhaps billions, of "climate refugees" with nowhere to go—a recipe for planetary social chaos.

In the near future, human-caused climate change will continue to create natural disasters resulting in death and destruction. Extreme weather will haunt us more frequently. Food and water scarcity will ensue. In larger-scale calamities, there will be confusion, lawlessness, and social chaos. Local or neighboring governments will restore order whenever possible; however, eventually, there may be so many emergencies that help cannot be provided.

On November 8, 2013, Typhoon Haiyan—with sustained winds of 195 miles per hour and massive storm surges—ripped across the Philippines, killing about six thousand people, leaving one million homes damaged, and displacing three million people. Haiyan was one of the most powerful storms ever experienced. Food and clean water became scarce. What came next is a microcosmic preview of future events that could occur on a massive scale. On November 14, 2013, the *Los Angeles Times* reported that five days after the typhoon: "panic was spreading and parched, hungry residents were resorting to increasingly desperate measures…Eight people were crushed to death when a huge crowd stormed a rice warehouse… Elsewhere residents dug up underground pipes and smashed them open to get water…Concerns grew about rampant looting and lawlessness… Armed assailants have been holding up aid convoys…Local officials said bands of looters, having cleaned out shops in Tacloban, were beginning to break into the homes of people who had died or fled the city."[2]

Dire circumstances are upon us. Unless we acknowledge our situation, we will be unwilling to face up to it. It is no longer impending; we have already arrived at the first station of our environmental apocalypse. CO_2 surpassed four hundred atmospheric parts per million (ppm) during 2013 and is silently, and for the most part invisibly, corroding the planet's

---

2 Alexandra Zavis and Sunshine De Leon, *Los Angeles Times* (Los Angeles, CA), Nov. 14, 2013.

ability to maintain its own healthy functioning. Every "ratcheting up" of the CO_2 meter points to death for elements of the Earth's living systems and to extinction for a portion of the entire biosphere. These results are foreordained and irreversible, and in a short amount of time, like radiation poisoning of a human body, the toll on plants and animals will be taken.

Something shocking occurred in the summer of 2007: the Arctic ice cap shrank 25 percent in one season. Until this happened, scientists were alarmed about climate change; after this occurred, most climate experts were aghast—their predictive models had projected a much longer time frame under the worst-case scenario. It became clear that other expected negative consequences were no longer hypothetical and would soon be revealed. Climate change was to be more rapid and devastating than anyone had predicted and was already in full process! This is no longer an issue our children and grandchildren must deal with. It is here, now, to haunt us all. Never, in the eleven thousand years since humans have settled into village life, had the climate destabilized—until now.

We have always been able to count on a hospitable climate to grow grains on the fertile continental central plains. We plant where the rivers have always flowed and the rain has always fallen. When rains are sparse, high mountain glaciers melt in the heat and feed the rivers, providing irrigation for our crops, fish for our tables, and clean water for drinking and bathing. Until now we never realized what a delicately balanced system this has been.

Recently increased industrial CO_2 production and fossil-fuel consumption has caused the average temperature to rise by about 1.5 degrees Fahrenheit. Notwithstanding the cause, this 1.5-degree temperature increase has opened the Arctic's northwest ice lanes for shipping, an inconceivable occurrence until now. Moreover, entire glaciers are disappearing while others are severely reduced in size. Massive feedlot cattle herds produce methane gas that is twenty-three times as climate-destructive as the same gas volume of CO_2-producing automobiles. Furthermore, vast peat bogs of permafrost in Siberia and Alaska are beginning to melt and release more methane into the atmosphere, a problem that could exceed all CO_2 fossil-fuel production.

The rainfall won't disappear—in fact, it will most likely increase—but it will more often fall in flood-causing volumes. Increasing planetary temperatures will allow the tropics to claim more land, but the adjoining subtropical lands will be hotter, causing additional moisture to be retained in the air and the rainfall patterns to change. When the temperature rises and changing rain patterns force farmers to abandon farmlands, formerly productive lands will turn to desert.

The entire world's food supply is grown on 3 percent of our planet's surface. This is the fertile land with soils built up over millennia in the floodplains and ancient lakebeds. These farmlands need rainfall to grow the food that feeds us all. The new rains, the harder rains, will come, but not to the fertile 3 percent of the planet. The water will move away, falling over the desert and the ocean. Because of reduced sequestered ice, the glaciers will stop feeding the great rivers, and the rivers will stop irrigating the downstream crops.

Literally billions of people have located their villages and cities because of the "life flow" that glacier-fed rivers provide in the heat of summer. A recent scientific study measured the outflow of more than one hundred of the world's largest rivers. This water volume has fallen by about 25 percent in the past fifty years. The rains have begun to change location; the glaciers have reduced their runoff. Future disruption and suffering is bound to occur when the water stops coming and the rainfall changes its location—flooding and drowning instead of feeding and nurturing!

Without immediate intervention, temperatures are predicted to rise another 5 or 6 degrees before the end of this century. If 1.5 degrees melts the Arctic's glaciers, transforms the rivers, and causes such severe weather disruption, what will 5 degrees do? Our best scientists do not know, but we do know the world is changing and will continue to change, bringing dramatic weather, more violent hurricanes and tornadoes, drought due to increased evaporation and relocated rains, ice sheets that slide to the sea, and rising sea levels. The Gulf Stream and other ocean conveyors will be negatively impacted, and ocean salinity and acidity will change, killing coral reefs—and on and on.

No one knows all the results. In fact, the potential consequences are unpredictable; however, we can be relatively sure that the food supply for a large percentage of the world's population will be disrupted, clean water will become scarce, political systems will be destabilized to the point of collapse; and perhaps a billion or more "environmental refugees" will be on the move, looking for a place that can support their families. Will these poor hordes be welcome in the wealthy northern countries? No, not when the wealthy will be facing their own chaotic disruptions, as will all people.

In this scenario, the barriers between rich and poor solidify more, becoming impermeable. When food and water are limited, those who control the resources are the ones who take the production for their own. The poor suffer first and struggle the most; ironically, they leave the smallest "carbon footprint" yet are the first to be displaced. Those living in low-lying tidal zones are displaced when unseasonal flooding engorges rivers and streams, sending clean, healthy drinking and irrigation water to the seas. Melting Antarctic ice sheets will further inundate the tidal estuaries with rising ocean water. Flimsy shantytowns next to rivers and oceans are found throughout the developing world. These are the first to go in floods, in higher tides, and in climate change–related hurricanes or typhoons.

The United States contains 5 percent of the world's population but uses about 25 percent of the world's raw materials. This group also consumes about 25 percent of all "goods" made and creates almost 25 percent of the CO_2 atmospheric poisoning. However, it will be the last to suffer and, perhaps, the last to cry out. Our government, chosen primarily by the financial elite, seems willing to sacrifice the many for the few. So far it has the power and influence to do so, an unhealthy situation to say the least—one that we hope to change, and soon!

To keep the science in perspective, I note that the CO_2 level remained below 300 ppm from the last ice age through the entire eleven thousand years that humans have practiced agriculture and settled in villages. Tree rings provide an excellent source for climate information, going back about twelve thousand years, almost to the end of the last ice age. Astoundingly, ice-coring techniques are able to measure atmospheric CO_2 and provide other climate information going back at least eight hundred thousand years, and sediments on the ocean floor provide a continuous record of climate change, tectonic plate movement, and ocean drift, reaching back *five million years.*

Since atmospheric pollution began during the industrial revolution about the year 1800, we have steadily increased the atmospheric CO_2 level. It is currently above 400 ppm, well past the safe level. Our best climate-change researchers have concluded that the life we have settled into—our cities, our crops, our animal husbandry, the air we breathe—will be irrevocably damaged, and to some extent destroyed, by ongoing CO_2 levels greater than 350 ppm. Yet, we continue to ignite fossil fuel into our atmosphere, converting liquid oil to gaseous carbon with little hope of reducing the level to 350 ppm.

Both wealthy and poor nations recognize the climate-change debate to be a critical one. What is not yet recognized is that the time for debating has expired, just as *we* have begun to expire without realizing the insidious, irreversible consequences of our actions. It's not a political issue; it's not an economic issue; it is a physical reality of the planet we live on, the only one we've got. CO_2 levels at 400 ppm, and rising, will obliterate the world we know and result in an altered Earth—one that we will not recognize; one that cannot support a population of seven billion humans.

Oh, the Earth will survive and regenerate; it always has. But what a hellacious process for our children to be put through, and what a price for our grandchildren to pay! All the forests and the animals, all the lakes and streams, all the oceans and coral reefs, all these things and more will partially die.

CO_2 atmospheric increase and climate chaos is not the only potential disaster that we face. There are even more immediate threats. Our prehuman ancestors learned about fire, most likely the hard way. Coals were captured from lightning fires, campfires became ubiquitous, some individuals "played with fire," accidents happened, and people died while learning how to live harmoniously with fire—how to accept fire's gifts without hurting themselves or others. Nuclear bombs, nuclear power, nuclear waste—all are examples of us humans playing with fire. If we are not more careful, fire will destroy us.

Radioactive fallout can sicken our species and destabilize Nature. Children learn about fire from personal experiences. As we become a wiser adult society, we understand fire more thoroughly and learn to use it responsibly, so we don't allow our children to burn themselves; if we do not, we will suffer extraordinary consequences.

In March 2011, an earthquake-caused tsunami crippled four electricity-generating nuclear reactors at Fukushima, Japan. A massive release of radioactive material occurred, poisoning the surrounding communities. At the time of the accident, previously used, highly radioactive fuel rods from reactor unit 4 were temporarily housed in water-cooled pools. The structures housing reactors 1, 2, and 3 were damaged so badly that their fuel rods collapsed into the ground. The three reactor sites are so radioactive that they cannot be accessed for "cleanup" efforts.

Tepco, the corporation responsible for the power plant, is using seawater in a temporary attempt to control further nuclear reaction and additional radioactive release into the atmosphere; however, almost three years after the tsunami, quantities of this radioactive seawater are still being flushed into the surrounding ocean.

Reactors 1, 2, and 3 are very dangerous, but a potentially worst-case scenario is reserved for Fukushima's nuclear unit 4. At the time of the accident, its reactor was offline, and the fuel rods were temporarily stored in a cooling pool suspended more than sixty feet in the air. Although it is badly damaged at the time of this writing, the pool's cooling capacity is intact for the moment, but a future earthquake in this quake-prone region could collapse the badly damaged building and cooling pool, causing the worst nuclear disaster known to humankind.

In the final months of 2013, Tepco was attempting to remove the 1,331 fuel rods from reactor 4's high perch. This is a very dangerous proposition. Nothing of this sort has ever been attempted in the entire nuclear power industry's history. The fuel rods' containers are distorted from damage; there is debris in the water; some rods impede others. Each rod must be lifted by crane without getting stuck, breaking, or touching another rod bundle.

If anything goes wrong, "fuel pool criticality" could occur, causing events to spiral out of control. The pool cannot contain a nuclear reaction, which might occur if the fuel bundles get too close to each other. Were this to occur, it could not be stopped and might cause a meltdown with massive fires and radiation releases many thousand times greater than the Hiroshima bomb and the Chernobyl meltdown combined. Radioactive plumes could be spread across the entire northern hemisphere, poisoning farmland, crops, and cities.

Creating Our Planet's Physical Reality

Throughout the book I use various principles to discuss a core theme of our new story: *evolving human consciousness is a process that is advancing biological complexity on Earth.* One of these principles is that *our worldview and our behavior are creating our planet's physical reality.* In both positive and negative ways we humans have insinuated ourselves into the Earth's living systems. Our cultural values are recreating the planet's climate and, thereby, affecting the Earth's biological health by causing extensive negative repercussions. This process will dictate which species will go extinct and which will survive. Concurrently, we are deepening our understanding of reality and our appropriate place within our planet's biological and geological matrixes—a positive step toward Divine connection.

Human ingenuity has outpaced the evolution of human consciousness. How we perceive the world is creating the Earth's future; our attitude is shaping the planet's physical existence. What will our children's inheritance look like? Our level of appreciation or disdain for the Earth's healthy functioning is determining the extent to which we add more climate chaos, ocean acidification, irresponsible genetic engineering, nuclear waste, and species extinctions. Human suffering is the collateral damage. How extensive will this turmoil be? Our culture's current decisions are defining our legacy to future generations.

About a decade ago, a Dutch chemist named Paul Crutzen, who is also a Nobel Prize Laureate, wrote an article for the magazine *Nature* in which he elaborated his newly coined term *Anthropocene*, meaning "the age of mankind." Crutzen proposed that humans are currently affecting the planet's atmosphere, geology, and biology to the extent that we have created a new geological epoch, bringing a close to the current epoch, the Holocene, which started about twelve thousand years ago as an interglacial period that interrupted the last ice age. Since its introduction, the Anthropocene concept has been considered an accurate description by the world's preeminent geologic organization, the International Union of Geological Science, although no formal decision has been reached to adopt the term. Still, let's look at the variables involved.

Geologists study epochs by finding distinct boundaries in rock strata, layers delineating time periods that show a planetwide transition from one geologic condition to another. For example, there have been five major species extinction events; in each case, there was a massive die-off of the established life community on one side of a boundary and a proliferation of a new community on the other. Sixty-five million years ago, the dinosaurs went extinct along with a large percentage of all other life.

This was the last major extinction spasm prior to the one that is just beginning. The majority of life-forms that surround us today have developed since that time. To qualify as a new epoch replacing the Holocene, the rock strata being created today would have to reflect a significant disturbance caused anthropologically, that is, by mankind. Were we humans to disappear, all our buildings, freeways, cars, and bridges would leave little or no trace one hundred thousand years from now (a blip in geologic time).

What would show up in the rock strata record to define an epoch? The pollen records would show a dramatic change from great diversity two hundred years ago to the relatively few species like corn, wheat, and soy found today. Forest cover in the United States has been shrinking since European settlement began in 1630. Although relatively stable now in North America, this habitat loss is ongoing throughout most of the world and equates to species' extinctions that will show up in the fossil records being created today and in the near future.

Atmospheric CO_2 has risen dramatically to more than 400 ppm; this too is recorded in the strata. At the beginning of the industrial revolution, CO_2 concentrations were about 280 ppm. It has been eight hundred thousand years since CO_2 concentrations were above 300 ppm. Burning fossil fuels has provided the energy for industry to grow exponentially, decade after decade, but has also caused CO_2 concentrations to increase. It has been two and a half million years since atmospheric CO_2 was 400 ppm or greater; when this high CO_2 concentration last occurred, temperatures rose 18 degrees Fahrenheit, and sea levels ranged from 16 to 131 feet higher than today's level.

Repercussions from higher atmospheric CO_2 include increasing temperatures, climate chaos, rising sea levels, and additional extinctions. All this will be catalogued in the Anthropocene rock strata. The seas also absorb CO_2 from the air, which increases ocean acidity. As CO_2 molecules diffuse into the ocean water, they are mixed from the surface to the lower levels by the wind and churning waves, resulting in lowered ocean alkalinity. An estimated 30 percent of all ocean species are dependent on coral reefs. Coral's calcium carbonate shells are made from calcium ions and carbonate ions. The latter are chemically reactive with acids; more acidic water means these ions become much less available for the individual living corals to build their shells. This decline is well underway; coral reefs in the Caribbean Sea have declined by 80 percent since 1977 resulting in loss of the sea life nurseries that the reefs provide, in addition to oceanic flooding that will occur on all coastlines. Tellingly, each of the prior five major extinction spasms showed a "coral gap" in that epoch's fossil record.

Additional evidence supporting the Anthropocene concept relates to genetic engineering. Humans have recently begun to create new species in the lab. Where this will lead is anyone's guess; however, there is no denying that the *Homo sapiens* species is beginning to take a major role in biological evolution. Science fiction writers have envisioned many disastrous consequences, and science fiction sometimes becomes reality.

Medical writers predict numerous potential "cures" from DNA manipulation. Agriculturalists foresee heartier plants needing less fertilizers and pesticides while growing to larger sizes. Food animals are undergoing drastic manipulation as well. In salmon, for example, genetically combining one type with another creates an offspring that can grow to twice the size in less time than either original type. We are almost able to bring some extinct species back to life by finding or building their DNA structure, inserting it into living cells, and using surrogate mothers from a surviving similar species! An experiment by Spanish scientist in Madrid to bring back the Pyrenean ibex was almost successful; a living offspring was born, but died shortly thereafter. A similar project is being pursued to bring back the woolly mammoth.

What will be the eventual results? Will some human "designer" species escape to the wild and wipe out the native species? In some cases, yes, this is likely. Will this genetic experimenting bring new diseases along with the new creatures? Perhaps. The question is, can we create new species in an Earth-responsible way?

I reiterate that Natural Harmony is the mutually beneficial reciprocity that has been woven together over millions of years; building Earth's life community has been an intricate interrelational long-term endeavor.

A monarch butterfly in the pupa stage can only eat one plant, milkweed, which is geographically found hundreds of miles away from the monarch's adult "hangouts." So many pupae hatch on the milkweed that they could obliterate their host were they all to survive; however, the milkweed plant protects itself with a sticky sap. A large percentage of the pupae are caught in the sap and die. The survivors eat voraciously, eventually transforming into the beautifully colored monarchs. As the newly emerging butterflies leave the milkweed, they inadvertently step in the plant's pollen, which they spread to other milkweed plants. Many pupae die, and a great deal of milkweed is eaten away; however, in the final outcome, both species benefit.

How did this series of events develop? No one knows, but Nature is replete with millions of these relationships. How will our new human-made life-forms fit into this intricate scheme? I don't know, but I say this with confidence: while we continue our adolescent manipulation of Nature, it is essential that we be as careful as careful can be. Our current activities are now being preserved in new rock formations that will contain today's geologic record: the pollen diversity is declining and the CO_2 level is ascending. Perhaps when examined in the future, today's activities will also show a spike in exotic, manmade species followed by a rapid decline of all life forms—the legacy of an Anthropocene epoch.

Some geologists argue that geologic epochs should be much longer than the short period that we modern humans have walked the planet. In some respects, the Anthropocene concept is anthropocentric, another example of human arrogance in the face of geologic time scales. This may be accurate;

however, if we are indeed in a new Anthropocene epoch, when did it begin, that is, when did human geological impacts initiate a new epoch?

Not too many thousands of years after modern humans migrated out of Africa into Europe, all the megafauna, large land animals like the woolly mammoth and saber-toothed tiger, disappeared. Was this a coincidence? Not likely. After several hundred thousand years of living in what is now Europe, our *Homo sapiens* cousins, the Neanderthals, also disappeared ten thousand years after we "moderns" trekked into their regions. About eleven thousand years ago, we began agriculture, eventually converting vast stretches of open land, and later forestland, into cropland and cattle-raising land. More recently our industriousness and consumptive lifestyle decomposed and recomposed the atmosphere and oceans, beginning a major extinction spasm.

Hypothetically, natural conditions might have capped human population at about half a billion people in the Middle Ages; diseases like the black plague temporarily reduced the population in that period. Had similar diseases prevented population expansion, it is unlikely that the industrial revolution would have happened. If that had been the case, there would still be a relatively minor human impact; however, the population tripled in the next thousand years, science prevailed, and the production of "goods" proliferated. The human population is now fourteen times greater than it was after the plague.

I place the Anthropocene epoch's beginnings at the Hiroshima bombing, August 6, 1945. Technology, industry, and people's demand for more "stuff" had finally combined, garnering enough strength to overwhelm the Earth's ability to heal the year-to-year insults. In any case, the

Anthropocene epoch has become part of our New Creation Story. Finding Natural Harmony will require us to "see" the world in other than anthropocentric terms so that the Earth can once again be seen as sacred. If we are able to call forth the best ethical and creative qualities our species has to offer, our behavior will change. If so, we will be able to utilize existing technologies and yet-to-be-invented systems to dramatically lower our ecological footprint. This would still be an Anthropocene epoch, but not an anthropocentric one.

A corollary to a principle mentioned earlier (that our worldview and our behavior are creating our planet's physical reality) is this: *our internal turmoil is reflected in our external world—our personal dysfunction is projected out onto the world.* The climate is changing. While a few corporate-paid climatologists continue to feed us misleading disinformation that keeps politicians and public policy off balance, extreme climate events grow in ferocity. Radical weather events, including tornadoes, hurricanes, floods, massive dust storms, and droughts are occurring with greater frequency. Greenland's glaciers are melting into the sea at rates never before recorded.

Average temperatures have risen in each of the past four decades. The years 2000 through 2013 showed a faster rate of increase than the prior periods. The arctic ice cover has opened for the first time in recorded history; Antarctica is also sloughing off ice from land into the sea. The last century saw a six-inch rise in ocean levels. There are predictions of a *six-foot* rise in this century. Even a three-foot increase in water levels will flood out the world's most fertile rice-growing areas in Asia, creating worldwide food shortages. Climate change could more accurately be described as *climate chaos.*

We can expect many more major disruptions to weather patterns around the globe. In Montana, Glacier National Park has lost 90 percent of its glaciers; soon there will be none left. The Andes Mountains, the Tibetan Plateau, and other mountain glaciers are the planet's water storage reservoirs for the river systems that irrigate crops for several billion people. Their glacial melt keeps these water sources flowing in the hot, dry time of year. When the glaciers are gone and the rivers dry up, there will be no water for irrigation, and the people will go hungry.

How does this climate change affect us in the United States, Canada, and Europe? When grain crops fail in China and India, those countries must import food; the world's grain prices skyrocket, inflating prices for the crops and costs for consumers, thereby destabilizing world economies. The corporate, factory agriculture industry benefits at the expense of the average person. "Benefits" is an ironic term. This is a short-term, unsustainable circumstance that will soon come crashing down because worldwide recession is the ultimate consequence. The corporations will suffer with us all.

As the oceans rise, the land's water tables are falling. There are two types of underground water reservoirs: those that recharge from rains and those that were accumulated under ancient geological conditions, underground lakes and aquifers, with no source of replenishment. Most of the latter sources have already been consumed. For example, Saudi Arabia used up its nonrenewable water table in just twenty years of a crash wheat-growing program and has now returned to importing almost all its grains. The same depletion is occurring in the US Midwest, where the Texas panhandle has seen grain production plummet from a lack of water in its aquifer.

Of the renewable underground water, supplies can only last if they are pumped at no greater rates than they are restored. This is not happening. Farmers with new technology, deeper drilling, and more powerful pumps are taking out much more water per year than nature can replenish. Water has become scarce. Water is the new gold. Corporations will devise business plans for any endeavor in which huge profits can be made. Controlling the world's water is no exception.

"Water wars" are inevitable and have already begun in some South American locations where water has been "privatized." When corporate "owners" of the rainwater raise the price to onerous levels, people will revolt. Political instability is bound to follow climate chaos. The Middle East has a critical shortage of water. Already a politically unstable region, it is becoming more volatile with each passing year.

Agriculture is dependent on topsoil. It took eons to form this priceless Earth asset: first, the mountains eroded to fine particles; next, plant life migrated from the sea, finding locations to "root," thereby holding the granules in place; plants died and added their carbon nutrients to the sandy base, imperceptible layer by imperceptible layer. Soil created over millions of years is measured in inches, not feet. By tilling in marginal areas to feed a booming human and cattle population, we are converting carbon-rich soils to dust. The wind blows it away to the mountains and oceans. Grasslands become deserts; an ecology that took many thousands of years to form is reduced to sand dunes in just a few decades.

This "desertification" is occurring all over the world. As with your own skin, soil is a living membrane, full of microorganisms that facilitate crop production. When the membrane is peeled away, the Earth is wounded. Human and livestock populations continue to expand while the soils needed to feed us are in decline. The result is food shortage and political instability; ultimately, chaos ensues.

There will be many other planetary changes; for example, overfishing the world's oceans is now collapsing the world's fisheries. As detailed previously, we are causing a massive extinction spasm that is likely to eliminate the majority of Earth's species. In short, our production and consumption cultural priorities are creating a diminished world.

Future Generations

It is also true that our species has the capability to create beauty and love. We do it all the time. Humans are now responsible for the changes that are determining the Earth's physical well-being: the health of the air, the water, and, consequently, the biosphere. This creation story is about finding Natural Harmony before it is too late for our planet's health and our children's future. The Iroquois League comprised five different nations and was bonded together by a constitution that was used as a model for the US Constitution. Their decision-making looked seven generations into the future to anticipate what effects their present actions would have on their distant offspring.

With today's technology and exponentially rapid changes, it is harder to see forward seven generations; however, we are not even looking after the next generation, our own children, or our grandchildren. How many of us can see even three generations ahead? No one, not even one expert, knows the state of the world fifty years from now; however, this does not absolve us from considering potentially damaging consequences of our choices: climate chaos, planetwide social unrest, potential nuclear war, devastating nuclear reactor accidents, irresponsible genetic manipulation, and species extinctions. It has now become essential that we make it a priority to understand the future we are creating and base our actions on these insights.

If we are to succeed, it is necessary that we "see" ourselves differently and acknowledge our "shadow side" as a culture. Our treatment of the planet is abusive, and the consequences are becoming abusive to our own children—and to their children. In our current trajectory, we are a planetary pathogen that is putting other life into an irreversible descent, to the point where much of it will eventually disappear from Earth. Change cannot appear before we recognize that there are repressed, unconscious influences driving our cultural behavior. Although unique and special, we humans are not the chosen ones. We are a clever animal species, perhaps too clever. We have no dominion over other animals—no longer, not in the New Creation Story.

Cheap fossil fuel gave us the automobile; the automobile gave us suburban houses and strip malls, far from the city or the town center. Villages lost vitality; downtowns became vacant; communities collapsed. With the rise of corporate farming, shops and homes became separate, as did farms. Corporate food became cheap and unhealthy, "shipped" across the states and the oceans, to the point that the consumer today has no clue where his food originates. Clothes and toys have become just as anonymous. In the suburbs, community culture gave way to television culture. In Los Angeles the auto and oil companies conspired to dismantle what had been a good mass-transit trolley system to make way for more cars and more profit; similar injustices occurred in other cities across America. In the isolated suburbs, with no stores nearby and a commute to work, one family car is not enough. After the Second World War, starting in 1945, a watershed year with a world population of 2.5 billion, the automobile literally redesigned American life. Now its poisonous byproducts continue to reconfigure atmospheric chemistry.

Villages encouraged social interaction and interresponsibility. Everyone knew the old lady with no family that needed help with groceries. Folks were aware of the harmless village idiot and protected him on the street from insensitive outsiders. Most of the food came from nearby, and we knew how it was grown. After 1945, with the corporate-imposed "American dream"—a single-family house with two cars in the driveway—community life in America began to disintegrate. Homeless people and territorial gangs eventually claimed the inner cities. Main streets in small towns, including Clearwater, Florida, where I grew up, lost their stores to shopping malls and began to decay.

As is often the case in Nature, our disease points to our cure. Frequently one will find an antidote growing in close proximity to a poisonous plant.

How do we recreate community, the antitheses of independence and isolation? Farmers' markets are springing up everywhere. Locally grown, often organic foods are being offered, but that's not all. Take a few minutes to compare the interactions between people at "supermarkets" with those at a farmers' market. You will find, as researchers have, that the interactions among individuals have multiplied manifold at the farmers' markets. The atmosphere is village-like and sometimes even festive. It's not corporate; it's personal and fun.

Our ancient roots are those of community, not isolation. Farmers' markets feel better for good reasons; they are in our cultural memory bank; they are our history. The fluorescent lights and long aisles of plasticized, artificial food is not something we really want, but like all things corporate, rooted in sophisticated advertising campaigns and images, we can be manipulated to accept what is not healthy for us, physically and emotionally. Autos are case in point. Billed as the epitome of success, independence, and well-being, they have in reality created the exact opposite: isolation, reduction in community, increased meaninglessness, and planetary decline unlike anything humans have ever known.

When I give talks that include this New Creation Story as a topic, an audience member often suggests that we adopt the Native American or other indigenous cultures' Earth-honoring philosophies, maintaining that returning to these values would solve our problems. My response: yes, it's vitally important to incorporate this wisdom, but no, it's not sufficient. In various past times, philosophers have articulated similar positions: native people are "noble" and modern urban people are destructive and dysfunctional. Usually there is judgment involved: the "good" native verses the "bad" city dweller.

In school fifty years ago, we used the term "noble savage" to indicate a romantic appreciation for native lifestyle and philosophy. Not all indigenous people treated their neighbors with respect; however, those who did not live harmoniously with Nature did not survive. Chief Seattle's noble statements (in a speech written by a white man for the chief) were applauded; as well they deserved to be. I often refer to "Native American Earth-honoring philosophy" to indicate respect for "Mother Earth." There were some noble tribal societies, but they were confined to particular conditions and circumstances, bound in place and time. There was no television to display the "goods" they did not have; no motorcycles or four-wheel-drive trucks; no vacuum cleaners or washing machines; no rapid-fire transport to exotic faraway places—in short, no modern "stuff" to tempt away the native nobility.

Unfortunately, we are past the point of no return. Let's not ask too much of any social group, noble or otherwise. To some extent, we all crave what we don't have. Craving is an excellent distraction from meaninglessness—that is, until we find that "stuff" cannot provide meaning, only distraction.

Even though I haven't seen Sophia in a dream for a long time, I sometimes feel her presence. I was walking in the city, snow on the ground, thinking about my young children and feeling good about Christmas. There were carols wafting in the clear, cold air. For no particular reason, my mood suddenly shifted to thoughts about money and buying presents. The kids expected it. Abruptly stopping, head bowed, my left hand pressed against my cheek, I asked myself: "What is it that seems so off?" Feeling heavy, I sat on a nearby bench. Amid the public din, an answer pressed from an unknown source into my mind, as though Sophia were talking to me in my dream: "Consumerism has become our life; economic success is admired while relationships with one another are ignored. The corporate system is using us for fuel—burning us up. It constricts us. Intuition and creativity are stifled. Sensuality, artistic endeavors, and gentleness are swept away. All this is founded on more and more production, consumption, and accumulation. This is not life; it's more like producing death."

I've become more familiar with death over the past two years since being diagnosed with prostate cancer. I'm building my immune system so that my own body can "doctor" itself. But it adds an "edge" to life—gratitude for each day. So far the cancer is low-grade; I've decided to track it using the "active surveillance" method as opposed to rushing into surgery or radiation treatment. Allopathic medicine is good at diagnosis. Waiting in the doctor's office for some tests, I was paging through a magazine with its colorful advertising arrays; a thought floated into my aware-ness: "I don't have to buy the stuff; I can do whatever I want. Manufacturers and advertisers have their freedom to present me with these things; I have freedom to take them or not, right?"

The nurses were passing by; I leaned back for several min-utes. At that point I heard a thought coming from deep within my body: "Our society and collective psyche have become so *hypnotized into believing that we have to have more in order to be more, that there really is very little freedom left to choose not to be manipulated further by the sophisticated messages from Madison Avenue that bombard us constantly—ubiquitous in the public airwaves. Greed drives our society. To realize this is to be liberated, to find choices. As more people choose freedom from greed, concern for others and generosity will eventually take its place. The economic system that has polluted the air and water will change. Life's success is measured by appreciation and gratitude, not by accumulation and power." I somehow felt lighter. Instead of being concerned about my cancer, I was just thankful for the medical people, showing up every day to help others.*

Death is a sagacious advisor. I have a good friend whose wife passed away two days ago. They were an inseparable couple, still very much in love after forty years of marriage. Jack suffered monumental losses: his life partner, his beloved lover, his intellectual companion, his co-author, and his spiritual mate. Death brings us face to face with our core values. Learning more about where we have come from will help us to know our essence and give both life and death more profound meaning. Our human story starts all the way back at the creation of the universe and informs us about the present moment—our gains, our losses, our intimacies, our loves, and the Earth that created us.

CHAPTER 3

THE COSMOS BURSTS FORTH

We Humans are so intimately related to the physical planet of our birth that our Creation Story must include cosmic origins, our Sun, and our planet—if there is no Earth, there is no human being.

It was a time before time began, in a place before there was space, in a circumstance of which we know nothing—a total mystery: the ineffable magic-moment-before-the-Big-Bang. Suddenly the seed cracks open: there is a bursting forth infla- tion, more powerful than the mind can grasp. This blasting- out conflagration is an energy field containing preatomic quark particles under incomprehensible pressure and force. Almost immediately quarks clump into protons and neutrons;

from the first second to the third minute of the Universe's inflation, these particles aggregate into hydrogen and helium nuclei; however, it would be almost 400,000 years before enough electrons are combined with these nuclei to produce the atoms that are responsible for the Universe's first light—a cosmic glow.

As the Universe expands, hydrogen nuclei collide and fuse, forming more helium; in a several-step process, a stable form of helium appears. Tiny amounts of lithium also came into being in this initial "neucleosynthesis" process, and a few other trace elements. Soon after the Big Bang, the Universe had inflated sufficiently to reduce pressure and particle collisions to the point that this hydrogen-to-helium fusion could no longer occur. At this stage the Universe's total mass was composed of almost three-quarters hydrogen and one-quarter helium. All other heavier elements, except the traces mentioned, would be produced later in the cores of the stars and in their final supernova death throes.

This hydrogen-helium gas world then began a primordial bonding. Gravity attracted the atomic matter into clouds, which eventually coalesced into clusters. These massive pregalactic atomic structures continued to build more profound coherence. After 300 million years, these clouds of matter had collapsed into innumerable, separate galaxies. Stars were born within the galaxies. Under further gravitational compression, this starmatter collapsed into stars, began to brighten the heavens; under unfathomable pressure inside each star, hydrogen once again began colliding with enough force to fuse into helium, giving off excess energy that manifests as incredible heat and light.

Once upon a long time ago, our Earth's journey was born, with all its potential grandeur: in a time when the Milky Way Galaxy had existed for more than nine billion years, a star exploded in the heavens. That star had lived for billions of years, burned up its energy, and lost much of its mass; and now, in a final flaming conflagration, it spewed innumerable star-made atoms into space. There were no eyes to witness it. Not long after this Great Spewing Forth event (that is to say, not long in cosmic time), a large amount of this liberated "star-stuff" began to coalesce, collapsing in on itself from gravitational attraction— heavenly Eros in action. The unfathomable increase in density and pressure from these primordial particles pressing together in cosmic bonding raised core temperatures, igniting a new star, our Sun. Other atoms and molecules from the exploding star came together in a similar coalescing to form a much smaller body with fiery, molten rock at her center, but without the size or pressure needed to ignite its entire mass. The Earth was born. Both Sun and Earth appeared in the celestial firmament about four and a half billion years ago. Imagine all that cosmic time without the Earth—then, almost suddenly, its manifestation.

This creation event is age-dated from meteorite fragments that are somewhat older than 4.5 billion years, which is supported by dating techniques based on the oldest lead deposits on Earth.[3] Our Moon has the same composition as the Earth's surface; and evidence from 2011 seems to indicate that its interior is viscous, not solid, and radiates tremendous heat. That discovery would support the hypothesis that the Moon formed in the same manner as the Earth, with Earth having captured most of the available iron and other elements and, therefore, forming a larger gravitational field. An alternate theory is that, shortly after the Earth's formation, a large meteor hit Earth and blasted debris from the newly formed planet into the sky. Soon thereafter this material merged together from gravity and collision, beginning its Earth-orbit as the Moon.[4] Our story continues:

The Earth was a fiery ball of molten rock for the first hundred thousand years or so, after which time the surface cooled and solidified into a terra firma crust. The oceans and atmosphere followed not long afterward, making Earth capable of supporting life, although there is no remaining evidence of life from this early period. Any progress in the "coming to life" endeavor may have met with cataclysmic demise when a half billion years after Earth's formation there was an event called the "Late Heavy Bombardment." Close-orbiting material left over from the formation of the Sun and other planets in the solar

3 W. L. Newman, "Age of the Earth," Publications Services, USGS (July 2007), http://pubs.usgs.gov/gip/geotime/age.html.

4 J. W.Valley, W. H. Peck,, E. M. King, and S. A. Wilde, "A cool early Earth," *Geology* 30 (4) (April 2002): 351–354. See also: N. Dauphas,, F. Robert, and B. Marty, "The Late Asteroidal and Cometary Bombardment of Earth as Recorded in Water Deuterium to Protium Ratio," Icarus 148 (2) (December 2000): 508–512. doi:10.1006/icar.2000.6489.

system collided with the Earth. This event lasted for about two hundred million years, perhaps evaporating the oceans and blowing away any early atmosphere. Life that may have developed was lost. Ocean water and atmospheric gases that evaporated away in these collisions were partially replaced by water and gases contributed from the colliding comets. Earth's volcanic eruptions also brought forth water vapor and other gases that added to Earth's new oceans and atmosphere.

Our story has begun with the Universe coming to life from an indescribably dense, energy-laden bursting forth, an expanding moment that is the seed for all known material existence. It continues to unfold from that birthing to the present—a new moment in cosmic existence in which humans are the most complex beings known.

We are not better, not smarter, not healthier, and not more important than the other large-brained mammals, including the whales and elephants; however, by virtue of self-reflective consciousness, humans are, for this Creation Story, the most complex. Through ingenuity and invention, humanity has become a partner in almost all the Earth's processes: changing the atmosphere and its climate; causing the demise of a large percentage of Earth's life-forms; creating new living organisms through genetic engineering; turning wild animals into zoo inhabitants and, consequently, changing their future physical forms; damming the mighty Amazon, thereby modifying the entire Amazon basin's flora and fauna and beginning the demise of this massive wilderness. Amid this destruction there are positive developments: for example, humans are adding more coherence through the very process of deepening awareness—evolving human consciousness.

An Urge to Complexity

More than nine billion years passed before the Universe produced the Earth. Eventually our planet developed consciousness that could observe this grand creation. Behold the self-reflective conscious human mind. We are the cosmos contemplating itself. Odds are that there is other similar consciousness on distant planets or moons; if so, whether carbon based or formed from some other essential element, the elapsed time from the Big Bang to life's appearance might be similar, given that the elements needed to form life must be created in a second- or third-generation star.

In November 2013, the National Academy of Sciences held a meeting and published its proceedings, including a study estimating that there are 11 billion Earth-like planets in the Milky Way galaxy alone, and our galaxy is just one out of billions in the Universe. These planets orbit in solar systems that provide them with a temperature zone that could support liquid water and allow for the type of life that exists on Earth. Both reason and intuition tell me that there are many billions of life-forms on these planets; to believe otherwise, to think that we are so special that no other "intelligent life" exists in the Universe, seems extremely arrogant.

We are part of a "complexification" process—the very same process that has unfolded in a systematic way for 13.8 billion years and has brought us to this place in our Creation Story. Is it a place in "time" and "space"?

We don't know yet if our normal human perception of time and space are real, that is, are consistent with some absolute "universal reality." Part of our story is to acknowledge our current perceptual limitations. In retrospect it is easy to see that our knowledge was comparatively limited prior to, say, the fourteenth century—before Thomas Bacon, Isaac Newton, and their peers. I have no doubt that in a few decades our current understandings will seem just as primitive. Human awareness is in transition, as it always has been; we are one of Earth's experiments, engaged in advancing biological consciousness—an experiment in which the new Ecological Epoch is now offering us an opportunity to expand our intimacy with the Creative Source.

Recently we have learned that the Universe is expanding at a particular rate, that is, the galaxies are speeding away from their origin and from each other. The Big Bang was an inconceivably powerful energy conflagration; initially, it formed hydrogen nuclei from subatomic particles; then helium was created. All was held in affinity through gravity. If this attraction had been slightly less, the atoms would have flown apart so rapidly that they would not have coalesced into the massive clouds that formed the galaxies.

This event happened only once in the Universe's history. Because of the physics and chemistry involved, it could only have happened with these particular circumstances. Conversely, if gravity had been slightly stronger, the galaxies may have formed; however, they would have collapsed back together in a great contraction, perhaps into the original "singularity." It is theorized that this balanced expansion speed is so precise that the universe could not have survived if the speed varied by a minute fraction of 1 percent.

Was this precision a coincidence? Not likely—but how could it have occurred? There are many theories available for this debate. Perhaps the Big Bang's original singularity exploded outward umpteen times, and without the "proper" energetic velocity, it continually collapsed back—until that one magical occurrence when, after billions of years and trillions of attempts, just the right conditions existed to permit the next stage to unfold. Alternatively, perhaps in some process unknown to us, the expansion speed and gravity are aspects of the same "force field" that are created together and must balance with one another by definition. What actually happened at the Big Bang remains hidden in some greater wisdom implicit in the Universe itself—and in that mysterious sacred darkness that existed in the magic moment just before the Big Bang.

Cosmology is the purview of the very large. One's mind must expand to its full capacity to comprehend our solar system, the Milky Way galaxy in which our Sun and Earth reside, the Large Magellanic Cloud (LMC), a nearby galactic neighbor, and all the many mind-bending cosmic phenomena: black holes; the vast 13.8-billion-year existence; the Big Bang origin; and much more. What does it mean when I say that the LMC is part of the "local group" of galaxies, or that it is about one-tenth the Milky Way's mass and is actually a satellite of our galaxy? The LMC is about 160 light-years away. Can one's mind comprehend a light-year, the distance light travels in one year at 186,282 miles per second? Or is it truly unfathomable? Can a person "enter into" a connection with the galaxy or the cosmos? Rational thought is the most likely portal to such a vast territory; however, this "thinking" mode is often a "cool" experience. It is not sensual or emotional—not typically passionate. So where can we get passion for the cosmos itself? How can one fall in love, into intimacy, with something so vast, so nebulous; something that we have just begun to understand in any depth during the past few decades?

Once in a while, I'm fortunate enough to be on a mountain, no lights, and stars blazing. These are our stars, our Milky Way galaxy, as they are the only ones that can be seen without a telescope. It is always an awesome sight—meditative awe. My mind tells me that I am part of what I'm seeing, but I can't quite make that cognitive leap. The distance is so far; the cold is so absolute, the logic is so new; the Big Bang is so strange. I can't escape the irrational "magic" of that event. What existed before it? Cosmologists tell us that the galaxies are all expanding away from each other in such a way that each is at the center of the expansion! What in the non-world is outside our expanding universe; what are we are moving into as we expand? If it's not the existing universe, and it cannot be by definition, then what? But still, the awe of it all, the profundity; my senses can feel its depth a little, up on that mountain, even if my mind can't wrap around the vastness.

For me, all this relating is more readily focused on the Earth, not the cosmos. Let Earth relate to cosmos; how much cosmic relating can be done by a normal person? I can't touch the stars; they are awesome to see, yet there's limited access. Sight is the only one of my five senses that comes into play. Most Earth-based things can be accessed through intellect, the senses, and emotions; cosmic things are learned only through intellect and, to a limited extent, emotions. Years ago I had an impactful dream that I was stuck in "space." There was no life, no warmth, no comforting beauty; all those protective qualities that the Earth offers were missing.

Upon waking, I found myself dramatically affected by my dream; I felt hollow and depressed. This demonstrated to me the nurturing qualities of the Earth and brought home my appreciation for the Earth's warmth— the coziness our home planet provides. Our story continues:

> Our planet was created along with the solar system and given the tools to come alive. Earth was formed from a first-generation star that cooked up many of our planet's elements in its interior cauldron, including life-building carbon. More chemical elements were made in the explosion of the star's final death throes. All this creativity was needed to provide the materials that compose the Earth—a thin rock firmament floating above its molten core. Heat convection forces move continents, form mountains, and open oceans. Interior forces create atmosphere and, ultimately, provide water for the dynamic hydrological cycles necessary for all life.
>
> Innumerable intertwined processes led to life's appearance 3.8 billion years ago and are still essential for life to evolve and prosper. Earth has a dependent state of relatedness with its Sun. Earth-life created the chlorophyll molecule that, in turn, facilitated photosynthesis. The Sun's photons then provided energy for multiple new life-forms, a proliferation that brought forth new complexity. Life has continually become more complex since inception. This is an essential raison d'etre for Planet Earth. Humans and all other animal species are designed so that each

might successfully reproduce. The Earth houses this intense reproductive proliferation within a system that is powered by the Sun.

We humans exist as a process of the Earth that is, in turn, utterly dependent on the solar system. Time passes. The Universe expands, unfolds, and reveals itself. What will transpire in the future is "implicate," that is, unknown and yet to be expressed. What life-forms will survive on Earth? Like the water patterns in a mountain stream: which way will the flow bend around an obstacle; which large rock is strong enough to hold its ground and force the flow to detour; which boulders will eventually get washed away, removing a long-term impediment; where will the uneven bottom grab hold and produce a vortex in the flowing uniformity; where does the bottom fall away to produce massive falls and turbulent waves?

And yet, all this turbulence foaming in and out of existence is moving toward the same destination: down the path of least resistance, through the river gorge to merge with the seawater, from where it originated. Our Universe seems to be the same, a flowing process moving inextricably toward greater and greater complexification before it eventually...

The Magic behind the Big Bang

The "Big Bang" theory of the Universe's origin can be examined in a scientific manner, starting at the moment of manifestation; however, the moment just preceding this event is totally unknown to us—we have no way to conceive of it. It is the "magic moment behind the Big Bang." Cosmic complexity appears, manifest as our expanding Universe.

Just as confounding as this magic, preexistence moment is the question: "What is it that the Universe is expanding into?" As the outermost galaxies fly apart from nearby neighbors at almost the speed of light, thereby expanding the Universe's space, what boundary are they crossing over? What is outside that leading edge? Given that the Universe is *everything* there is, and this "outside-the-leading-edge" place is not yet in the Universe, then what is it, if anything? Is it nothing? How does one describe this "no-thing"? It is a second unknown place that is not describable, another magical place not in our Universe.

Is it perhaps the *same* magical place from which we started in the moment preceding the Big Bang? In any case, we humans are not yet smart enough to comprehend these two magical quasi-"existences." They belong to the Tao, the Great Spirit, God, Goddess, Creative Source. They are the known Universe's bookends that, like God in the *Tao Te Ching*, it is impossible to describe. This reality points to a necessary, essential humility in human thought and behavior. Our New Creation Story still originates from the same place that it did in 600 BCE when Lao Tzu said, "All things arise from the same source, subtle wonder within mysterious darkness." All these years later, although we know a lot about what is occurring between the bookends, we must remain in humble respect of this wonder and sacred darkness, the Creative Source.

This story is all about coming to know Natural Harmony and behaving in concert with this preexistent, integrated, universal form. The discovery process includes a discussion about how the cosmos "works," what it is, how it is unfolding, how the galaxies formed, and how the stars and solar systems with planets and moons came to be. What amazing new information has come to us since Nicolaus Copernicus declared that the Earth was not the center of the Universe in 1544 (although the Greek Aristarchus had taught this eighteen centuries prior to Copernicus, he was later ignored).

The last fifty years have given us space exploration, moon landings, and satellites circling distant planets with cameras whirring. In 1977 Voyagers 1 and 2 were launched with a mission to explore a number of planets; eventually they were to leave our solar system and send back data about "deep space," the region beyond the influence of our Sun. As recently as 1979, scientists learned from the Voyager flights that Jupiter's moon Io has numerous active volcanoes; prior to this, it was thought that only the Earth had volcanoes. In 1989 Voyager discovered that Neptune has winds of 1400 mph and a moon, Triton, with geysers that emit nitrogen gas. Voyager is still discovering things that no one ever imagined; our understanding of the cosmos continues to change and grow. Deep space penetration has never been accomplished. After thirty-seven years of flying past the other planets' orbits, Voyager 1 has flown beyond the solar system's outside edge and become the first human-made thing to escape the Sun's influence.

We now know that there are billions of other stars, many with planets and moons, that have similar conditions to our Earth and are likely to contain life. Naturally, that life is intelligent, because all life has intelligence and functions within a cosmic "unfolding" process. Is there self-reflective consciousness on some of those celestial bodies? Most likely! Is the universe "our Universe" in the sense that the Earth is "our planet"? This is an existential question worth pondering. It needs no resolution. We live on this Earth-home of ours. We wouldn't do well anywhere else, certainly not yet. Earth's life began 3.8 billion years ago. Our human journey has just begun.

In many respects, we Earth-animals and Earth-plants are all simply an unfolding process of the Earth. As when a small acorn becomes a giant oak, we humans are incipient potential having taken form. Humans, by virtue of self-reflective consciousness and our creative power, have a different niche. Perhaps more privileged, certainly not "better"; however, with privilege comes responsibility. This is the lesson we have recently learned and are trying to integrate into our species-wide behavior. We are now sharing the shaping of the geologic and biologic Earth. We have become a partner in Earth's life formation—and in Earth's death throes. Life on other planets will follow different processes and articulate life differently. The Milky Way galaxy is a child of the cosmos. Our Sun is nestled within the Milky Way's multibillion star interactive gravitational field. Our solar system survives for the moment within this balanced equilibrium. Our Earth is absolutely dependent on the Sun for our energy, biology, and healthy functioning. We humans are children of this Earth.

Mother Earth

The cosmos is something so vast it is almost unfathomable; the Earth, however, is right here with us, providing for us, nurturing us, and inspiring our life journey, as indigenous people intuitively knew from their interactions with nature (Mother Earth). We are the Earth's children. Perhaps it is a useful metaphor to say that the Earth is the daughter of the Sun. If we humans let the Sun and the Earth mediate with the other stars, the stars with the galaxies, and the galaxies with the universal Whole, we will be better able to sensually embrace our fellow Earth-beings; it's harder to be intimate with the Large Magellan Cloud than it is with a flower-filled meadow. In our story:

First, there is an origination miracle, an outward explosion— a God and spirit moment. As the inconceivable heat and pressure reduced slightly by cosmic expansion, preatomic particles combined to form hydrogen atoms, some helium atoms, and small quantities of lithium. These coalesced into massive clouds that collapsed from gravity, forming incipient galaxies whose hydrogen, under increasing pressure and density, ignited and formed stars—a fusion process driven by hydrogen atoms colliding and fusing into helium, giving off heat and energy. Other, heavier elements such as carbon, nitrogen, and oxygen formed from further fusion processes within the star, primarily in a "red giant" star: its life cycle complete, the first-generation star eventually exploded outward as a "supernova" event, which forged the heavier molecules and created all the remaining elements in the periodic table, all down the line to uranium.

Our Sun formed by capturing most of the emancipated star-stuff in one region, but there was elemental "stuff" left over; colliding and merging, sweeping together materials and finding their own concentric orbits, the remaining material formed Earth and the other planets. Life begins; humans are created—all this is full of God and spirit from the inception. Because human life is sacred, and we contain spirit, and we came from the hydrogen atom, then hydrogen and everything else in the entire process must also be sacred. It is all imbued with spirit. Matter is spiritual! We are mistaken to think that the sacred is about human activity. It is this, but it is also much more pervasive. Realizing this, we see the world differently, and our actions reflect our new understandings. Science has been about matter; religion has been about spirit. There had been no common ground until recently. When we "get" that matter is imbued with spirit, these disciplines become reconciled, and we perceive Earth's sacred nature.

CHAPTER 4

IN THE BEGINNING

Man's general way of thinking of the totality, i.e. his general world view, is crucial for overall order of the human mind itself. If he thinks of the totality as constituted as independent fragments, then that is how his mind will tend to operate, but if he can include everything coherently and harmoniously in an overall whole that is undivided, unbroken and without border then his mind will tend to move in a similar way, and from this will flow an orderly action within the whole.

—David Bohm, *Wholeness and the Implicate Order*, 1980

Imagine in your mind's eye the early Earth, seven hundred million years after its formation. Two hundred thousand years of meteorite bombardments had recently ended. It was 3.8 billion years ago: peeking above the oceans, there was little more than volcanic islands, many the size of Hawaii, with desolate lava rock surfaces barren of life. It's a challenge to comprehend the life process that brought us from lava islands to the magnificent abundance that surrounds us today. How could this transformation have happened?

In the Bible's first chapters, an omniscient and omnipotent "God" decided to form the world; worked hard for six days, making all it components; then rested to admire His accomplishments on the seventh day. In biblical times there was little factual data for an individual to use in contemplating life's origins. The creation story in Genesis is fascinating when considered metaphorically (which is done in detail in this trilogy's Book Two). Interestingly, ancient Greek philosophers from the Axial Age, notably Thales of Miletus (sixth century BCE) had intuited that life arose spontaneously from water as a medium, not from an intervening God. In the fourth century BCE, Democritus proposed that tiny particles called "atoms" were the building blocks that combined in different ways to create matter. The famous Aristotle opposed Democritus, taking the position that all life is imbued with a "life force," a quality that distinguished life and separated it from inanimate objects. This idea was called "vitalism." Without scientific tools to validate either hypothesis, and with the rise of Christian doctrine, these early intuitions fell by the wayside and were mostly forgotten.

Surprisingly, it was not until the 1860s and 1870s that the Frenchman Louis Pasteur and the renowned Charles Darwin shed additional light on the origins of life with the speculation that life arose spontaneously from organic chemical processes that were exposed to energy sources. ("Organic" simply means that the element carbon is involved; carbon is the one atom essential for all forms of life on Earth.) In 1922 the Russian Aleksandr Oparin refined the hypothesis, proposing that a "primordial soup" could form in bodies of water. This was an increasingly complex mixture of organic molecules, perhaps in tide pools and other wetlands, which, when exposed to sunlight or lightning under perfect conditions, could begin chemical reproduction processes that are the initial steps needed for life to form.

In 1929 the British biochemist J. B. S. Haldane took these ideas further, speculating that complex organic molecules might have become self-replicating, thereby transforming inanimate chemicals into the first life. In the 1970s serious consideration was given to the possibility that life could also have arisen in deep ocean geothermal vents, which have the necessary heat and energy source in combination with the chemical complexity required. The early conditions in which life evolved may not exist on today's Earth, and researchers have yet to produce life from chemicals. Today's ongoing research uses the "primordial soup" concept as its foundation. In our new story:

> *Life began as a series of more and more complex chemical steps, perhaps millions upon millions of trials building toward the eventual appearance of self-replicating chemicals. Initially there is a synthesis of complex molecules; favorable conditions allow for their concentration. Over millions of years, random*

chemical processes experiment with encapsulation and organization into innumerable molecular structures, some of which become self-replicating, allowing further complexity and stability of form. Afterward, competition arises between the successful molecular forms. Natural selection begins. It favors those with superior survival traits. This chemical evolution demonstrates a drive toward greater complexity: a step-like, ongoing process that eventually produces life. By way of emergent complexity, biology is born.

The boundary between "life" and "not life" is not at all clear-cut. It is more like a continuum than a boundary. While writing these pages, I often remind myself to remain cognizant of the "deep time spans" contained in these creation and evolution events. Just one-tenth of one billion years is one hundred million years. Researchers have found actual fossils, that is, fossilized bacteria, dating back more than three billion years. This is the oldest direct evidence of life that is available. Indirect evidence, including bacteria in rocks, dates back to perhaps 3.5 billion years ago, and geochemical indications that life existed go back as far as 3.8 billion years. It may have taken a few hundred million years of molecular chemical experimentation for life to emerge, but emerge it did! There is, however, still scientific dispute about the precise timing for when chemicals "came to life." For our story, approximate time frames will suffice.

Of more importance is the personal and cultural impact that this "Earth history" has on our individual psyches. None of the information presented in these pages was known one hundred years ago. Dating techniques for both the Earth's formation and the beginning of life have only been available since the early twentieth century. New understanding about radioactivity helped the cause. Radiometric dating uses radioactive substances that decay from one form (isotope) into another over a known period of time. The original form's unstable nucleus spontaneously decays, over a known time frame, into a new (daughter) substance. By examining these particular radioactive elements that exist in some rock formations containing fossils, and determining how much of this decay process has run its course, a researcher can age-date the fossil. For example, uranium decays into lead over a long period, providing information from billions of years ago for the rock layers involved.

Just as the idea that the Earth is the center of the Universe has tremendous effect on a person's psyche, so too does the belief that the Earth's age is about six thousand years old. In the 1600s a Catholic Church Archbishop, James Ussher, analyzed the Bible's book of Genesis and determined that the Earth was formed in the year 4004 BCE, which was about 5600 years prior. This determination was accepted and promoted by the church, although this was at odds with observations from a century earlier by philosophers and scientists, including Leonardo da Vinci, who calculated a two-hundred-thousand-year time frame for the formation of some layered rock outcroppings that were being formed from local riverbed sediment.

It was not until the 1920s that scientists proposed that the Earth may be hundreds of millions of years old, perhaps even the astonishing ancient age of a billion years, based on radiometric dating. Our recent mind-boggling understandings of deep time place us in a new and different embrace with our planet's dynamic processes and its living history. Life's genesis and, consequently, the "human condition" are now scientifically known to be different than previously believed for all human history, save for the most recent few decades. It's now important that our New Creation Story, "who we are" in relation to our beginning, incorporates these deep-time discoveries so that we comprehend our appropriate place on the planet, among its many other creatures.

Mind, Logic, and Imagination

This story includes many important developmental variables, but nothing more essential to the human story than the dance between the masculine-leaning *logos* and the more feminine *intuition*. Like *yin* and *yang*, balance is an essential element in harmony. Humans have had little *need* for the history of life on Earth—until now! Why have we recently learned so much in such a short time? Perhaps the information has been made available on a need-to-know basis. The Earth is suffering; many species are withering away. We need to know that this is occurring and why, if for no other reason than to find context for our human existence—to reorient ourselves. We are becoming informed in order to develop the skills necessary for our children to survive.

What a gift this rational mind is: its investigative reporting, its capacity for awe, its ability to generate abstract thoughts! Yes, our inventive genius has built the bomb, has polluted our children's air, has cut down the forests, has tripled the human population in my lifetime, and has initiated a horrific decline in the existence of other species. Concurrently, the human mind has discovered the origins of Planet Earth, the history of life, the evolution of human consciousness, and the structure of subatomic particles. How fascinating to contemplate the Big Bang, the Universe's 13.8-billion-year history, and Earth's coming-to-life story.

The thinking mind is surely an important life miracle. Four billion years into our 4.57-billion-year creation story, not a single tree had evolved. There were no animals with eyes to witness the dramatic mountain landscape. This was not a warm, fuzzy world that could sustain a human being: only stark, stony plains with no soil, no place for plants to grow, no haven for animal life. Yet, our incredible self-reflective, logical mind can take us back to appreciate this evolving grandeur. There are even films to show us what this particular Earth-time-space was like. We have learned that the past is not gone. Using our minds and fertile imaginations we reconstruct creation with our story:

The Creative Source ushered life into being. Time passed. New life-forms appeared by the multimillions. Who or what was the Creator? Perhaps "Great Spirit" imbued all life. Maybe "God" wove all living things together; or it might simply have been "Nature." But it is not necessary to use words, especially as God is beyond words. The description is in the creation. Just look closely at what exists around you—and appreciate it. If we just do this, we will feel the loss each time we realize that a species has blinked out of existence, never to be experienced by our grandchildren—or anyone. Life is expressed in such profusion, such magnificence, that the Creative Source and this awesome Creation deserve respect and gratitude from us!

The great monotheistic religions—Judaism, Christianity, and Islam—are correct to appreciate God through His manifest forms. These religions came about prior to knowing Earth-life's history. Notwithstanding all our knowledge, we still cannot explain the moment before the Big Bang or the amorphous Creative Presence behind the scenes that set all this munificence into motion. That initial moment, that Big Bang Flaring Forth, is God-Presence—a mystical God Moment. Everything that has happened since has been creation in process. Many synonyms apply; one is Nature expressed as Natural Harmony. For more than four billion years, the entire Precambrian period, life's emergent complexity was limited to a profusion of microscopic forms.

The religions were right to be in awe of God's creation. It was not a six-day process, but perhaps this time frame can stand in as a metaphor for a 4.57-billion-year process. An unnamable God created Nature aligned in Natural Harmony. But there is no resting on the seventh day, not yet at least—or perhaps the metaphorical seventh day has not yet arrived. Humans are a special species, as are all the animals; we are a work in progress, stumbling our way toward realignment with Nature, trying to learn from our recent blunders.

The Garden of Eden is another useful metaphor. As we have seen, it took almost four billion years to grow this garden. Metaphorically speaking, our journey out of Eden began at the time we branched off from the other primates, about seven million years ago. Later, sometime in the last two hundred thousand years, we bit into that symbolic apple. Was it when we first gained self-reflective awareness? So yes, call this creation process by any sacred name: *Elegant Creation from the darkness beyond human awareness.* All our present-day science was unknown when the Bible was written. We still have no clue about what stands behind Creation. But we now know a lot: the Creator God of the Bible, the One working arduously for six days and nights, that God is Earth's life-forming process. That God is Nature manifesting as Natural Harmony.

Earth-Life Emerges

Continuing with our story's chronology, we can generalize and say the first life-forms emerged three to four billion years ago. Interestingly, in these early stages, evolution seems to have been a very slow process. As mentioned, the earliest fossil evidence of life is from single-celled bacteria dating to more than three billion years ago; however, even these cells are complex structures that would have taken long time frames to develop, so we can assume the process had been in motion for most of the one-billion-year period since the end of the Great Bombardment mentioned above. It took a long time for chemicals in the early primordial soup to come to life, "learn" to replicate, form cell walls, and develop all the other complex systems needed to survive and evolve into different microorganisms. All this is the excruciatingly long process (at least in human time comprehension) required to create new single-celled beings.

There has been active debate about the possibility that bacterial life on Earth was "seeded" from meteorites that landed on Earth after traveling through space. That is a viable possibility, but Mars is perhaps the only good candidate for a "donor" planet within our solar system; the physical possibility of seeding from beyond our solar system is thought to be highly remote. In any case, bacterial life, whether seeded or not, began to evolve with the protection, support, and encouragement of our home, Planet Earth.

We are all familiar with the organisms called "bacteria." In modern life they are most often associated with common colds or infections; sometimes their beneficial qualities are mentioned, for example in digestion, but not often. Interestingly, the period we have been discussing (starting 3.8 billion years ago) is not named after bacteria; rather, it is named after a different microorganism called "Archaea," and the geologic period spanning about 1.3 billion years is known as the Archaean geologic eon. Its name is derived from ancient Greek meaning "beginning" or "origins." These tiny, single-celled critters are so similar to bacteria that, until the 1970s, they were scientifically grouped together. Major differences in characteristics emerged. Archaea contain genes. Compared to bacteria, they are more closely related to multicelled organisms that developed five hundred million years later. For this entire 1.3-billion-year period, bacteria and Archaea microorganisms were the only life. Adding Earth's seven-hundred-million-year prelife time period, our story has thus far covered close to half the Earth's 4.57-billion-year life. Two billion years into our story, we have single-celled bacteria and Archaea, that's all!

Life on Earth has displayed a biological imperative to become more and more complex over vast time spans. This "emergent complexity" is the driving force behind evolution. For example, approximately 2.1 billion years ago, microorganisms became multicellular. What an achievement! Some of our best research scientists, the brightest scientific minds, are working in labs around the world attempting to explain life's origins and to recreate the simplest life from chemicals—without success. This new and incredibly complex multicellular organism is a spectacular advance toward more complex life. Let's take a minute to reflect on our story as it has unfolded to this point:

The Universe burst forth with indescribable energy; all was contained in an expanding, incredibly dense energy caldron—let's call it the "Universe Womb"; also contained were subatomic particles, photons, neutrinos, electrons, and quarks. The caldron expanded further in this unfathomably dense, multitrillion-degree temperature, the particles combining to become hydrogen and helium atoms. With more expansion, clouds of these atoms, attracted by gravitational forces, broke into affinity groups that became galaxies; further gravitational attraction differentiated each galactic cloud, collapsing it into billions of individual entities (like snowflakes, each unique) precipitating out into stars. One of these stars within our Milky Way galaxy burned for billions of years, creating in its core most of the elements that exist on Earth. Having spent all its hydrogen fuel creating helium, excess energy, and heat, that first-generation star cooled, exploded, and disintegrated out into space; the especially intense energy created in this supernova event formed more heavy elements needed for life on Earth.

Some of this exploded star-stuff, attracted together by grav-ity, coalesced into a second-generation star, our Sun; residual material too far away to be captured by the Sun merged and melted together into the early Earth—soon augmented by bombardment with additional residual debris attracted by the Earth's gravity. During much of the Earth's first seven hun-dred million years, its surface was frequently bombarded with rocky debris, rendering it inhospitable to life. After most of this residual material had been absorbed, oceans, volcanic islands, and atmosphere provided an opportunity to brew a "primor-dial chemical soup," using the elements, carbon in particular, "cooked up" in the exploded star's core. Thus began an unre-lenting reconfiguration, chemical experiments by the billions, eventually leading to self-replicating life.

These life-building processes took place in tidal pools, the border areas where the ocean meets the newly forming volcanic land masses; additionally, in the open ocean there were hydrothermal vents, deep ocean openings where magnum-escaping heat rises from the ocean floor. These vents provided an energy source and the elemental building blocks needed for life—concentrated heat and chemicals, all in close proximity, able to self-replicate.

Much of this early life developed in waterborne microbial mats—lay-ers of bacteria and Archaea microorganisms held together, layer upon layer, by their slimy secretions to form large mats. Living in these combi-nations provided symbiotic advantages. Waste from one organism could be utilized as food for another; the mat formed a protective home with a specialized environment; various layers had different chemical composition, allowing new life-forms to emerge within the mat ecology.

After more than 1.7 billion years as the only life-form, single-celled microorganisms became more complex and created multicellular beings. It took more than half the Earth's 4.57-billion-year existence to produce this remarkable new life-form. (For more information see Appendix 1.)

Eukaryotes and Photosynthesis

But our story is getting ahead of itself. Let's back up to a period several hundred million years before multicellular life existed. At this time there appeared an ineffable, mysterious, unexplainable transition, a further complexity of single-celled beings called "eukaryotes." There exist today three phylogenetic branches, or domains, of evolutionary descent: bacteria, Archaea, and eukaryotes. The early eukaryotes were single celled, like all other life of the period; however, their appearance is critical to our story because they are the microform that eventually evolved into all of today's animals.

What distinguishes eukaryote cells are the specialized functions that are contained in enclosed units called organelles (akin to organs in the human body). They are complex structures surrounded by membranes. Organelles' nuclei contain genetic material. Mitochondria (originally independent bacteria before being "captured" and incorporated into the eukaryote cell) are employed in the eukaryote's energy production; for example, some mitochondria have chloroplasts that help to convert sunlight into energy.

Eukaryotes have a host of other substructures that function as the cell's "organs." The best evidence indicates that early eukaryotes were plentiful perhaps 1.85 billion years ago. They may have emerged much earlier in microbial mats but did not proliferate until later, after developing forms that could utilize oxygen. Although there are still many microscopic eukaryotes known as "protists," all larger life-forms, including fungi, plants, and animals, are also eukaryotes. Because their cells have nuclei with chromosomes that contain their genetic material, cell division can occur through sexual reproduction, whereby genetic material from each parent is recombined. This provides the offspring with more genetic variety, facilitating biological diversity and evolution.

Again our story must backtrack a little so that we don't ignore an Earth creation that also transformed the planet: photosynthesis. This was made possible by the chlorophyll molecule. For more than two billion years, the Earth's atmosphere was created from volcanoes spewing gases: water vapor, ammonia, methane, sulfur, and CO_2. This resulted in an atmosphere composed primarily of nitrogen (formed from volcanic ammonia reacting with sunlight), CO_2, methane, and sulfur dioxide. There was no free oxygen at this time, as it was not found in volcanic gases. As the Earth cooled and volcanoes erupted, water vapor condensed into oceans.

Early life developed in this milieu. Then, about 2.4 billion years ago, as a result of several hundred million years of photosynthesis, oxygen began to flood the atmosphere. Oxygen was toxic to most life-forms. This period occurs at slightly more than half of our planet's current 4.57-billion-year life. A key point here is that, because of their complex form, eukaryotes had greater energy needs than other living beings. Oxygen was the fuel that could chemically facilitate these requirements; however, its availability in abundance was essential in order to supply enough energy for eukaryotic proliferation. And proliferate they did—eventually becoming dinosaurs, redwood trees, and elephants.

Bacteria and Archaea, without the advantages of organelles and internal complexity, continued to thrive and create many successful new variations; however, they have remained less complex than the larger life-forms. It is noteworthy that, no matter what the fate of humans and other large mammals, the more basic life-forms, life's foundational core, are likely to survive any physical changes that result from the current, ongoing planetary insults. Mother Earth is intelligent!

As a general rule, plants get their energy directly from photosynthesis, and animals get their organic compounds, mostly sugars, indirectly from plants; hence, just about all sizeable organisms are life dependent on the photosynthesis process. Some smaller beings living near hydrothermal vents in the oceans survive on chemical energy, but this is unusual for present-day Earth-life. In addition, almost all animals depend on atmospheric oxygen as a fuel to power their cellular activity—breaking down organic compounds through oxidation.

It is estimated that plants create six times more energy from sunlight than all the energy used by humans (most human-produced energy is actually from carbohydrates produced by plants and sunlight; oil is an example). Naturally, sufficient oxygen in the atmosphere is essential to this entire cycle. Plants supply this oxygen as a photosynthetic byproduct. The entire system works together in harmonious union. Why? Because it evolved as one system over several billion years—millions upon millions of Earth's life experiments: trial and error, symbiosis, attraction, Eros, mysticism, and magic.

Photosynthesis is more than just the process that plants use to capture carbon from the air and utilize it to grow; it is much more—so much more that all large life-forms depend on photosynthesis to survive and grow! Green plants are photoautotrophs. They produce their own energy from light. Animals are not. We depend on the plants to capture carbon and store it in their bodies; we then eat the plants, or we eat other animals that have eaten the plants, and, through our digestion process, enlist the plant carbon in our bodily functions. This includes all our energy needs, cell replacement, and growth. Without the chlorophyll molecule, without photosynthesis, we would not exist.

Photosynthesis was a relatively early invention, coming after the planet's first billion years or so. CO_2 was much more prevalent in this early atmosphere than it is today. Cyanobacteria, also known as blue-green algae and blue-green bacteria, utilize photosynthesis. These early photon users date back to about 3 billion years ago and became so numerous from 3.0 billion to 2.5 billion years ago that a photosynthetic byproduct, the gas we call oxygen, began to proliferate in the atmosphere. This was a tragic occurrence for existing life-forms because oxygen was toxic for most then-existing life, which was killed off in a mass extinction spasm. This made room for new organisms to appear and take hold, organisms that could utilize oxygen in their metabolism.

Because they were more complex, eukaryotes had a higher energy requirement. As mentioned earlier, atmospheric oxygen was crucial in providing that energy and allowing them to proliferate in multiple forms.

In the period from three billion to two billion years ago, life experiments came and went by the millions. Eukaryote "protists" are unicellular or multicellular, but with a simple cellular organization. Early eukaryote protists had not yet developed specialized tissues, which came much later.

Miraculously, some of these multicellular eukaryote protists created an association with cyanobacteria by combining with them into new, hybrid organisms. Take a moment to contemplate: this integration is one of the most important events that has ever occurred on Earth. These eukaryote cells evolved into complex organisms that could produce their own energy after developing mitochondria organelles. Today's photosynthesis utilizes plant chloroplasts that evolved from this coming-together. All our present-day plants and animals are offspring from this marriage.

This remarkable transformation occurred when eukaryote cells entered into a symbiotic union (called endosymbiosis) with cyanobacteria cells, initially by ingesting them for food. Some of these ingested photosynthetic bacteria survived and were able to reproduce themselves *inside* the large eukaryote cells. This environment was protective for them; they took up residence. Over millions of generations, most of the organelles' DNA migrated to their hosts, and they became fully integrated. Through further evolution these bacteria eventually became the chloroplast organelles that are essential for plant photosynthesis. One fascinating observation to this story: it is theorized that all photosynthetic plants have evolved from *one* "mother" cell, a particular merging of an individual eukaryote with a cyanobacteria cell. This specific combination was such a superior advance, providing huge competitive advantage, that its offspring superseded all other contemporaries.

How does photosynthesis work? Photons are energized particles emitted by the Sun. They have no mass. By using chloroplasts in its cells, the plant is able to convert photons into energy and, thereby, power photosynthesis, which is a chemical process. Some of this energy breaks apart water molecules to obtain electrons that are needed to convert CO_2 into organic compounds. Through its leaves, a plant obtains the needed CO_2 from the atmosphere. (For a more detailed explanation, see Appendix 2.)

The Cambrian period started 542 million years ago. From the time when life on Earth began 3.2 billion years prior to this period, all life was microscopic, that is, all living things were microorganisms—no exceptions. One would need a microscope to see these tiny creatures. As the microscope was not invented until 1674, even we recent humans were unaware that these invisible creatures existed. We are not independent of them; interestingly, we now know that separate organisms that we host on and within our bodies vastly outnumber our own cells. Many of these microorganisms serve important functions that help us; for example, bacteria on our skin aids the immune system by preventing invasive toxins, and bacteria in our gut helps to digest our food. It's not surprising that we humans have an incomplete understanding of our own origins, given that we have been so ignorant about our kinship with organisms that are keeping us alive. (For more detail see Appendix 3).

Our New Creation Story provides a synopsis of what-on-Earth happened during the planet's first four billion years:

Several events, three in particular, changed the course of life on Earth. First, bacteria were unable to grow into large cells, most likely because they did not have membrane walls and, therefore, could not provide enough energy to support increased size. However, one form of bacteria in particular, photosynthetic cyanobacteria, was remarkably successful; it created oxygen as a by-product of its metabolism, proliferated, and eventually "oxygenated" the atmosphere. Second, some Archaea cells evolved into eukaryote cells with cell membranes instead of rigid walls; third, these eukaryote cells eventually became complex organisms that could produce their own energy after incorporating mitochondria organelles that were able to directly utilize the Sun's energy.

These cells were larger and more complex than all earlier life; they needed oxygen to fuel their much higher energy requirements. Given the newly oxygenated atmosphere, they were able to proliferate. With eukaryotes' emergence, the cellular structure that could support larger species was now in place. Blue-green algae and blue-green bacteria utilized photosynthesis; eukaryote protists cells were much more complex than bacteria and contained the potential, given a photosynthetic energy source and oxygen, to create new, larger, and more complicated lifeforms. Cyanobacteria provided this resource; thus, these two types of living beings combined, allowing eukaryotes to expand exponentially.

The photosynthesis and eukaryote chapter of our creation story is so impactful that, over time, innumerable trees eventually appeared. Trees are not built from the ground up; they are not made from the ground but rather from the atmosphere; their *bodies are constructed from carbon extracted from the air. Land gives them a place to "root," a position to grow. Although the minerals from soil are important to a tree's development, the tree does more to create soil than it does to use soil.*

We humans are composed of complex eukaryote cells, which were invented by the Earth eons ago; as such, we are living embodiments of the past. If we forget where we came from, we cut ourselves off from our source and, as a consequence, drastically reduce our own creativity. In *Requiem for a Nun*, William Faulkner said, "The past is never dead. It's not even past." The past is present, living within us and available to inform our cells and our minds. The more we know of it, that is, the more we see ourselves as we really are, the more we understand our origin, and the less likely it is that we will continue to destroy our Earth household.

The Cambrian Period

The Cambrian period creates a cornucopia of life tumbling into a Garden of Eden. Enter a new host of characters in our play—little more than half a billion years in the past. It is 542 million years ago that macroscopic animals, those large enough to be visible to the human eye (had there been such an innovation at the time) blossomed in profusion. Was there a reason? As mentioned earlier, life seems to have an urge for "expressing" in continually more complex ways, which I refer to as "emergent complexity." What a delight: animals with hard shells appear, and so large; soon thereafter, we find animals with vertebrae. All were still residing in the oceans, primordial lakes, and wetlands; another ninety million years would pass before plants colonized the land on a large scale. And colonize they did!

Eukaryotes' versatility allowed multicelled life-forms to arise, not just through mutations but also independently of one another; these included fungi, plants, algae, and slime molds, among others. Green algae are plants that live in the water. Land plants are called embryophytes. They include trees, ferns, and flowers, in addition to other green plants. These plants are thought to have colonized land about 450 million years ago. Embryophytes are all complex eukaryotes that get their energy from photosynthesizing the Sun's light. Their food comes from CO_2 in the air; they use photosynthetic energy to break apart molecules, utilizing the carbon and returning oxygen to the atmosphere. At this stage in our story:

Life has been created by star particles drawn together in erotic embrace. Almost four billion years have passed since Earth's formation. Because so much new variety occurs in the next 542 million years, our story now begins a whirlwind tour through time. The Cambrian period lasted from 542 to 485 million years ago. The period begins with atmospheric CO_2 levels at perhaps twenty times today's 400 ppm, putting it in the neighborhood of 7,000 ppm. As we know, green plants utilize CO_2.

In the ocean, invertebrate animals appeared about 525 million years ago, part of the dramatic diversity found in the Cambrian explosion. Life as we know it had started to blossom.

It was this blossoming that, during the following one half billion years, created our world: the glens and meadows, the cathedral redwoods, mountain flowers, deer and elk and bear, birdsong, great apes, and, eventually, a most recent arrival—humans.

Please stop here; take a deep breath along with the Earth's rotation and our orbiting ride around the Sun; all the while our Milky Way galaxy flies outward in rhythm with the entire Universe—about sixty-three million years pass, and we come to the end of the Cambrian period.5 The time had come for large animals.

In the seas and lakes and wetlands, life had already developed and thrived in profusion; however, at this time only microscopic plants and animals existed on land. The challenge in migrating onto land was how to keep from drying out—a life-and-death problem. Over the next many million years, microbial mats—thick masses of ocean-borne plant material that also housed many tiny animals, all entangled in massive "rafts" and interacting in symbiotic cooperation—may have learned to survive at the water's edge. Using the mat's ability to retain water and protect the organisms living within, some plant and animal species could migrate further inland. There was no soil at this time because there were no organisms large enough to provide the carbon content. The Earth's surface was barren

---

5 Notable from this period was a marine animal category called Anomalocaridid: graceful, fast-swimming carnivores that sometimes grew to between two and seven feet in length.

rock or weathered sand created from erosion. Still a stark place indeed after more than four billion years! However, by the end of the Cambrian period 485 million years ago, most of today's animal phyla had come into being.

Please take another deep breath to allow a *40-million-year* Earth cycle, starting 485 million years ago, to run its course.

By 445 million years ago, many new invertebrates had appeared, including early corals and starfish. An additional 25 million years passed, and by 420 million years ago, vascular plants and millipedes had colonized land, becoming the most complex nonmarine animals that had ever existed. In the ocean the first fish with jaws marked an advance in complexity.

With the next breath we look at another *sixty million years.* Although land plants such as four-inch-high club mosses and some animals lived on land 420 million years ago, a landscape recognizable to us humans did not arrive until about 360 million years ago near the end of a period called Devonian. By this time we find ferns, horsetails, seed-bearing plants, the first *trees*, and the first insects.

Burrowing animals helped create soil, a mixture of minerals and organic matter, by loosening the particles and providing suitable "beds" for plants and trees. Trees used the soil to "take *hold"; roots provided stability and drew water and minerals upward to the canopy of photosynthesizing leaves. Using the high concentration of atmospheric CO_2, large trees prolifer-ated, which led to a new crisis for life on Earth. There were so many large trees near the end of the Devonian period (370 million years ago) that their presence changed river courses from straight to meandering, and their growth sequestered so much carbon from the air that less sunlight was trapped. This reduced the surface temperatures that had prevailed in the pre-Devonian's high-carbon "greenhouse" atmosphere, eventu-ally resulting in an "ice age" cycle.*

Slowly, deeply inhaling and exhaling, other Earth creation cycles unfold over the next *forty million years.*

By 330 million years ago, during a period called Carboniferous, there were tremendous amounts of carbon sequestered out of the air and into the foliage of large primitive trees—so much that coastal swamps began creating coal. Land vertebrates appeared, and, in the ocean water, early sharks appeared as well. All this occurred about one hundred million years before the dinosaurs. The lakes and rivers were ruled by huge fish, rhizodonts, that grew to twenty feet in length and fed on sharks; while laying their eggs in the water, land vertebrates also became prey. By 305 million years ago, insects with wings take to the sky, some almost two feet in wingspan. There are many amphibians, and the first reptiles appear. Coal-forming forests proliferate; and because of massive tree populations, the atmospheric oxygen levels reach their all-time highest levels, much higher than today.

Let's stop again to contemplate time's vast spans; allow *sixty million years* to pass before your mind's eye, bringing our story to 270 million years ago. Can anyone really comprehend such an expanse?

From 270 million years ago to 251 million years ago, the coal-forming flora die out, and cone-bearing seed plants proliferate. Beetles and flies come into existence, and the oceans, lakes, and rivers flourish with new life. Then a disaster occurred for almost all this Earth-life that had become so prominent and diverse: 251 million years ago, the planet suffered the Permian-Triassic extinction event that wiped out more than 90 percent of all species! It had been 291 million years since the Cambrian explosion began; and now, life had collapsed in on itself. It was so devastating that many millions of years were needed for the remaining life-forms to recover and regenerate with new diversity.

Life on Earth has suffered a number of major extinction events—bad news for the beings that were thriving at those particular times. The good news is that life has always recovered in new profusion, with even more complex diversity than before the extinction, because ecological niches are made available for new life to refill. This is possible because prior life-forms, the former competition, have vacated the space.

The Permian-Triassic extinction from 251 million years ago has been called the "Great Dying" because it may have been the most extensive die-off ever; about 96 percent of marine species and 70 percent of land species went extinct, including the predinosaur "mammal-like" animals that ruled the period's land life. It is the only such event that included mass extinctions of insects. This biodiversity loss was so extensive that, even with many new ecological niches available, it took somewhere between ten million and thirty million years for the biosphere to recover and flourish. Experts are divided about what caused the Great Dying; however, potential culprits include increased volcanism, methane release from the sea floor, and meteorite impacts—any of which could have caused sufficient climate change to initiate the extinction spasm.

A number of major "extinction events" have occurred in the past 542 million years, which is the point when complex macroscopic life began to proliferate. These occurrences refer to large life-forms only, because it is so hard to measure effects on microscopic life due to paucity of fossil records. (A more detailed discussion about these occurrences is found in Appendix 4.)

But we're moving way too fast. Let's take another minute to *breathe*. Allow *forty-five million years* to go by!

Dinosaurs Dominate Starting 225 Million Years Ago

This is the time when dinosaurs seized their famous moment as the "big boss" on Earth. The moment lasted 160 million years, from about 225 million years ago to 65 million years ago. We have all seen, at least in photos, those giant dinosaur skeletons, standing twenty or twenty-five feet high. What is little known is the vast array of different dinosaur species. There were perhaps one thousand nonaviary species (and another nine thousand bird species). There were many more small dinosaurs than large; most were smaller than today's human beings. Where were our ancestors in their developmental process during this time period? That story begins with a subgroup of animals called Therapsids—members of a larger group called synapsids that includes mammals and their immediate evolutionary ancestors.

One of these early animal groups (a taxon, belonging to the Therapsids) was called "cynodonts" because of the animals' dog-like teeth. They predated dinosaurs by perhaps twenty million years. They developed into huge animals; however, as dinosaurs prevailed, all surviving cynodonts became smaller and somewhat "mammal-like," an indication of a dwindling habitat. They eventually went extinct during the dinosaur period, well before the major extinction event that killed off dinosaurs. Mammals appeared about two hundred million years ago, soon after the dinosaurs' reign had begun. Dinosaurs, large and small, were everywhere. They were carnivores and herbivores, fast and nimble runners. Dinosaur-like reptiles ruled the air (pterosaurs) and sea (plesiosaurs and pliosaurs). In short, these reptiles were ubiquitous; other animals lived at their mercy. Early mammals by necessity remained small and inconspicuous; being warm-blooded was an advantage for nocturnal activity and food gathering. The necessity to hunt at night may have helped warm-blooded mammals to evolve. It surely helped them to avoid the predominant ruling class and survive.

Another breath, another *sixty million years*!

By 165 million years ago, in the middle of the Jurassic period, conifer trees proliferated. Mammals were common but small in size; the first birds (all evolving from dinosaurs) and lizards appeared. About ninety million years ago, plants invented a most delicate accouterment—flowers burst forth! Many new insect varieties accompanied flowering plants. Dinosaurs continued to differentiate with new species; the famous Tyrannosaurs were born. At this point in our story, dinosaurs have dominated for 160 million years. Then disaster strikes again: the famous Cretaceous-Tertiary extinction, the one that ended dinosaurs' reign, occurred about sixty-five million years ago. Its cause is thought to have been a meteorite impact that occurred in what is present-day Mexico's Yucatan Peninsula. So much explosion debris was ejected into the atmosphere that, over a period of years, plants had insufficient sunlight to survive; the large animals lost their food sources and habitat. Birds evolved from dinosaurs in the famous Jurassic period, and some species survived this extinction, transforming over time into modern birds.

Approximately 75 percent of all species went extinct. After coexisting with dinosaurs for most of their 160-million-year reign, a new opportunity arrived for mammals. Previously, they were confined to small ecological niches or nocturnal activity to avoid those fierce predators. Now evolution was free to experiment! The climate was tropical; by about sixty million years ago, both plants and animals had developed many new arrays. The first large mammals arrived on the scene. They were the size of bears and small hippopotamuses, although unlike today's animals. Early whales populated the oceans after their ancestors had migrated from land onto the seas. By forty-nine million years ago, there was a change in atmospheric carbon, perhaps caused by a fern called Azolla. Its massive blooms extracted CO_2 from the air; huge quantities of Azolla blossomed in the Artic Ocean, then died and sank to the seabed, sequestering carbon in the sediments. Incredibly, over vast time scales, this process became important in removing CO_2 from the atmosphere, and transformed the climate from a "greenhouse" to an "icehouse" climate, resulting in various planetary glaciation cycles.

By forty million years ago, the climate was moderate, much cooler than before. Dinosaurs had been gone for twenty-five million years. Ancient mammals diversified and proliferated. In the oceans, after existing many millions of years, whales evolved further, creating new species. Early grasses became prominent. Ice caps began to form in the Artic as the Azolla and algae

proliferated, causing atmospheric CO_2 to fall from 3,800 ppm
to 650 ppm (compared to 400 ppm today), lowering planetary
temperatures.

Stop. Breathe. Allow *twenty million years* to pass, going forward to just five million years ago.

Volcanoes emitted CO_2 and other gases from the Earth's mantle into the atmosphere. There are several major processes that "fix" carbon and, thereby, lessen the amount of CO_2 in the atmosphere. The most familiar one is the biological cycle in which plants absorb CO_2 from the air and, through photosynthesis, incorporate the carbon into their own structures. Herbivorous animals eat the plants, obtaining carbon for their growth; carnivores eat other animals to gain needed nutrients. Over short periods of geologic time, the animals and plants die, releasing the carbon back into the air. Even long-lived trees decay over hundreds or perhaps a few thousand years. This is a short cycle in geologic time where processes are often measured in cycles lasting less than a million years.

In addition to the biological cycle, there is also a geological carbon cycle. Most of the Earth's crust is composed of silicate rock. As mountainous rock weathers over eons, the mountains erode. Silicate rock surfaces and its eroding particles are exposed to both CO_2 in the air and to rainwater. This chemical combination transforms the silicate rock into carbonate rock, sequestering carbon. The process accelerates with higher temperatures. For example, over a particular multimillion-year period, unusually high levels of CO_2 would result in higher atmospheric temperatures and a warming Earth. This situation would cause more rainfall and more "chemical weathering" from the combination of higher temperature and more rainwater causing more erosion; the result would be more carbonate rock formation. This "geological carbon sink" has much more influence over long time frames than the biological carbon cycle; it reduces unusually high CO_2, stabilizing the Earth's temperature, but can take millions of years to accomplish this task. Our story continues:

Reduced atmospheric CO_2 eventually created new planetwide glaciation cycles. Ice ages came and went in the period from twenty million years ago to five million years ago. In the northern hemisphere, mountain ranges formed from tectonic plate collisions; the mastodons and some other "ice age" megafauna came into being; forests became widespread, resulting in further CO_2 sequestration with levels falling from 650 ppm to 100 ppm, well below today's level. Horses and apes appeared. Our story has finally taken us to the Earth's most complex life—human beings. Our immediate ancestors arrived on the scene in modern form 200,000 years ago, long after our forefathers separated from the other primates seven million years prior. For eons prior to humans' emergence, life's evolution and transformation developed a foundation for this previously unexpressed complexity. These were not random events, coming and going without connection.

Although there were many dead-end branches in evolution, each successful stage was a necessary step in creating more complex life, including all the large-brained mammals. We are the bacteria; we are the early multicelled creatures; we are the eukaryotes; we are the dinosaur-era tiny mammals; we are our common ancestors, great apes; we are the hominids. All these ancestors are literally in our cells; as such, they are also in our cellular memories.

Our physical body contains a complex brain, a heart, and many other organs. We have muscles, glands, bones, and other components, all of which are in interdependent relationships with beneficial bacteria inside and outside the body. Consciousness is created not only by the brain but also from this entire gestalt. Personality is formed; emotions coalesce; individual worldviews are created both from inside our body and from external influences. Each person's unique psychological and emotional makeup produces his or her consciousness and also the "personal unconscious," including a pool of troublesome repressed or denied material.

An individual's personal consciousness, combined with his or her unconscious, forms unique personal "energy fields" containing nonphysical attributes—for example, Carl Jung's "anima" and "animus," which help to elaborate the variables that make up one's personality. In addition, each person has access to larger, transpersonal information fields—accumulated over generations. Complex, indeed!

Now, little more than a decade after the human genome was sequenced for the first time, scientists are beginning to understand how genes function; for example, they have uncovered about twenty-one thousand protein-making genes and almost thirty thousand genes that produce RNA. Each cell contains all these genes. Until recently it was thought that 80 percent of our genes were evolutionary dinosaurs, leftovers from prior developmental stages. Now we know that most, if not all, genes have an active function. Our DNA has millions of sites that act as switches to turn cellular functions on and off, each controlled by various proteins and chemicals. This is how a cell "knows" to produce a new liver cell or a blood platelet. Research scientists are creating an encyclopedia showing all the activity that occurs in our DNA strands. These processes bring to life our three billion DNA genetic "building blocks" and thereby regulate all new cellular development. Malfunction and damage to genetic material causes diseases, including many cancers.

The fossil ordering of species sometimes placed species in categories that current genetic analysis disputes. For example, from the fossil record whales and hippopotamuses were thought to be distant cousins. Now, genetics tell us they are very closely related. I am especially interested in this information because of a meditation I did about fifteen years ago—prior to the genetic analysis mentioned. Because all life began in the water and thrived first in the oceans, it was necessary for species that became land animals to leave the sea and continue to develop on land. After the dinosaurs, mammals became large, much bigger than those living today.

In my meditation, I saw a large, hippo-like mammal "returning" to the sea, and I realized that I was "seeing" a common ancestor of the hippo and whale at the beginning of this animal's transformation—a common descendent of both taking to the ocean to become, over millions of years, a whale. Recently, fossilized whales have been found dating back more than fifty million years, their bones showing residual, but functioning, small hind legs. Remnants from earlier terrestrial times, these appendages may have been used during mating before they faded out with evolutionary change.

CHAPTER 5

CREATION STORIES AND HUMAN CULTURE

Honor the past

Live in the present

Create the future

—Anonymous

When a society's creation story becomes too confining, it is unable to express its own epoch's most dire threats nor its grandest potential; in that case, the society's behavior is likely to reflect unhealthy choices. This is currently the case with our modern, unsustainable economic culture. A creation story serves to help us comprehend who we are and where we came from; our current stories, to the extent they are still influencing us at all, have allowed us to stumble on our way, to become lost in a meaningless universe. The Big Bang story of the creation of our universe from a "singularity" 13.8 billion years ago, and the Earth-life that followed, is quite recent—a good beginning point for a new story.

Other cultures, including some ancient and indigenous societies, have had grand visions of humankind's life purpose. Would it behoove us to revert to those worldviews as our guiding light? No, because they are not "of" our time and place. Change is occurring constantly. We are a people of a new epoch, and we need our own story—one that encompasses the wisdom that we moderns have realized. We are becoming a new species, one that is cocreating the physical world surrounding us. This includes deciding which living things will survive the current human-caused extinction spasm and which new life-forms will be genetically (artificially) created.

Our New Creation Story is meant to help locate each individual in his or her own sacred place and time. When focused in this way, we will have provided at least some guidance for relating to other people, to foreign cultures, and to Earth's many incredible creatures. Ultimately, we need a story that helps us find a new intimacy with the dynamic, living Earth itself. Our culture has adopted production and consumption as a social priority. Who you are is, to a large extent, defined by what you have. God is dead. Long live Stuff.

Modern science has done a great deal to destroy our prior creation stories, replacing them with scientism, a mechanistic outlook that does not need "spirit" to function. The Earth, the trees, the oceans, and their many creatures are all "seen" (perceived) as material "resources" to be consumed for our comfort and entertainment. In the process we have created a withering Earth. In this scientific age, the old creation stories no longer give us meaning; our society is, for the most part, devoid of the awe that creation stories offer. The virgin has been despoiled, the mystery lost.

It is very difficult to elucidate this [cosmic religious] feeling to anyone who is entirely without it...The religious geniuses of all ages have been distinguished by this kind of religious feeling, which knows no dogma and no God conceived in man's image.

—Albert Einstein[6]

Mysticism is no longer part of our collective focus. We are spiritually confused, partially from lack of a supportive creation story. One approach to restoring meaning is to articulate a creation story that fits our current circumstance, not one a few thousand years old or one originating five hundred years ago, rooted in a science that abhors sacred-Earth connections. It is our lack of connection that has allowed us to treat Earth as a smorgasbord of "raw materials" to be devoured in the pursuit of more automobiles and other nonessential "stuff."

To the extent that we still practice spirituality, we tend to rely on the philosophies of the Axial Age, those remarkable philosophers from 800 BCE to 200 BCE who gave us Hinduism, Buddhism, and Judaism—and later influenced Christianity and Islam. Our science and our unsustainable economic practices did not exist in these epochs. A New Creation Story is now required, one that incorporates our population density and our disease—consumption as a substitute for meaning.

6 *The Expanded Quotable Einstein* (Princeton University Press), p. 207.

The old name for tuberculosis was "consumption." It is a disease that slowly consumes its human host. We are suffering, and the Earth is suffering from consumption. Based on the urgency of earlier epoch's circumstances, the need to change has visited us humans often in the past. Now our destructive activities are calling for nothing less than our transformation.

We need a more profound creation story that adds value to our human endeavors, helps get us on a healthy track, and provides guidance for our culture's behavior. What does that look like? One quality is a return to the mystical. This includes our great-grandparents' Christian, Jewish, and Islamic mysticism, but also much more. It also requires respect for the Axial Age's "perennial philosophy" as well as all surviving ancient wisdom— but most important, we need Albert Einstein's science as sacred knowledge and a multitude of other newly articulated relational philosophies.

The most beautiful and most profound experience is the sensation of the mystical. It is the sower of all true science. He to whom this emotion is a stranger, who can no longer wonder and stand rapt in awe, is as good as dead. To know that what is impenetrable to us really exists, manifesting itself as the highest wisdom and the most radiant beauty which our dull faculties can comprehend only in their primitive forms—this knowledge, this feeling is at the center of true religiousness.

—Albert Einstein[7]

---

7   Albert Einstein, *The Merging of Spirit and Science*

All these many additional approaches will provide the individual threads to weave our cloth. We are searching for profound connection. For this New Creation Story to be useful, it must acknowledge the enormous challenges we face. In finding solutions the story incorporates not only hard-fact research science but also *mystical science*. This is where we find a flimsy veil dividing energy and matter. It is the mysterious moment, a numinous place in which energy coalesces into matter; matter, in turn, blinks apart, dissolving into pure energy, coming and going, coming and going. Energy becoming matter is creation itself. How does this happen? Why does this happen?

The wealthy Northern Hemisphere countries have built a relatively homogeneous society. Their citizens, for the most part, have similar perspectives. How we perceive the human condition, how we understand our origin, what we think about the mystery of creation, all these "big ticket" conceptualizations go a long way toward influencing our nation's social agenda. These are ideas, but they are powerful ideas. They establish how each of us defines ourselves and, consequently, drive our individual and social behavior.

You can't depend on your eyes when your
imagination is out of focus.

—Mark Twain

As mentioned and worth repeating, our *point of view* about Nature's importance, our *attitude* toward the Earth's creatures, our *perception* that the planet is a resource storage yard—all these are outlooks that shape the way we see the world and define reality. In our epoch these worldviews have become the tools that are sculpting the physical planet, creating changes that are occurring during a brief eye-blink in geologic time and in our story.

> *The Earth blinked. The humans came; the bomb exploded; the ice caps melted. Then something new happened: human consciousness expanded—Ecological Epoch consciousness appeared, inspired from the destruction. Consciousness flows like a river through time and cultures. There are eddies; there are stagnate lagoons, but floodwaters eventually come; the riverbanks deepen, allowing a new and vigorous flow toward inevitable destiny.*

In decades and generations to come, with more information and experience available, another creation story will replace the one related on these pages. As in times past, its coherence will depend on the then-current circumstances confronting society—the survival issues defining that particular moment's human condition. To be useful our new story must help to more deeply define our own life and relate our personal situation to all that is known. From the cosmos to quantum mechanics, we now *see* so much more than in prior times. This can be confusing, even paralyzing. Within this matrix our New Creation Story will help us to find balance.

One purpose of a creation story is to describe our origins to the listener: the beginning of time; where the world came from (the Earth, the heavens, the oceans, the trees); human beginnings; the human condition here on Earth; our relationships with other living beings (people, plants, animals); our destiny; and other "grand vision" concepts. This information orients society by incorporating what we know into digestible bites. The story necessarily includes our epoch's literal and metaphorical wisdom.

Creation stories emerge from a specific place in time and the imagination of a particular cultural moment. A story from ten thousand years ago in the Tigris-Euphrates Valley, before the wheel's discovery, will not include a chariot or an automobile. Likewise, the imagination, the consciousness, from early Christianity or Islam is insufficient to contain our current knowledge of the cosmos, the very large, or of particle physics, the very small. According to cosmologist Carl Sagan: "Hindus see the cosmos as having infinite deaths and rebirths…There are an infinite number of other universes, each with their own god…The Big Bang is our (western culture's) modern science creation myth."[8]

Just as Newtonian physics is useful within certain parameters but not in other ones, so too these earlier creation stories, although not "wrong," need additional depth and dimension to contain our epoch's wisdom and thus provide meaning to our culture. Science, too, is limited. In our modernity, the scientific "Big Bang" theory is our most currently "relevant story" to explain creation, becoming the first chapter in the scientific story.

But what existed before the Big Bang? What created this incredible event? You see the story still needs a miracle for it to be meaningful. Is the Big Bang that different from Genesis, in which God created the

---

8 *Cosmos*, Episode no. 10, "The Edge of Forever".

world in six days and rested on the seventh? The Big Bang hypothesis is a more sophisticated elaboration of what transpired *after* the originating event, incorporating a great deal of scientific knowledge; however, although it seems to be scientifically accurate, when we try to contemplate the inconceivable moment just prior, it is still a faith-based mystical event, this Universal Birthing from a singularity. It is also the initial event in our New Creation Story.

The "Big Bang" occurred, exploding outward from a singularity, the smallest point imaginable; the new Universe appeared—filled with the tiniest particles moving helter-skelter in quark-gluon plasma. The Big Bang expansion continued, and the Universe transitioned; the quarks were captured into protons and neutrons; innumerable hydrogen atoms appeared; in this intense energy and pressure, hydrogen atoms merged together, forming helium atoms, all of which existed in billowing pregalactic clouds. As gravity contracted the clouds, hydrogen and helium atoms were drawn closer together, providing raw material for the galaxies; these clouds become denser. Three hundred million years after the Big Bang, increasing pressure from the contraction precipitated trillions of stars into existence—hydrogen collided with enough force to fuse into helium, releasing the excess energy to burn, which is the fusion process that lights up the stars. Thus, the galaxies were born. Upon birth, each became a cosmological entity with its own massive gravitational force, each containing billions of stars, every galaxy a unique body with its own identity in the cosmos. Under intense pressure and heat, hydrogen and helium atoms continued to react inside the stars; helium transformed and many heavier elements, essential for life on Earth, came into being.

This is a story of an unfolding process, of chaos deepening into order. The story continues: because life cannot exist in the presence of the intense temperatures on a star, and the carbon needed for life is, so far in our story, trapped inside the original star, another unfolding stage is needed—and patience required. All stars have a life span; our Sun is about 4.57 billion years old and, based on the consumption of its hydrogen-helium fuel potential, is halfway through its lifetime.

The Universe is thought to be about 13.8 billion years old. The original star from which our Sun was formed exploded after its life span expired, spewing its contents into space; our solar system came into being when some of these now-liberated star elements attracted one another, coalescing together into a second-generation star, our own Sun. The planets in this system were also formed from "leftover" star matter, including the essential life-forming element, carbon—thus explaining carbon's escape from its formation in the first-generation star, and its presence on Earth. This multistep unfolding process is a recently realized scientific chapter that helps to form our creation story.

Creation myths usually include miracles. Is acceptance of the scientific Big Bang miracle any less arbitrary than believing in the many miracles that are included in the Bible or Koran? What the Big Bang is missing compared to almost all other creation myths is an explicit spiritual dimension, that is, a connection to a Creative Source, a Great Spirit, or a Sacred Integrating Force. Science provides information. Spirituality provides meaning. It is no coincidence that our Big Bang cultural creation myth comes from the imagination of a culture that is suffering from a deficit of meaning and fullness.

What is the Universe expanding into, anyway? Like all creation myths, ours is meant to allay existential fears by explaining the unknown parameters of our existence. The Big Bang is the beginning—the expanding Universe is the ongoing process. These are our bookends. As long as we don't try to think outside the bookends, outside the box, our fears are temporarily allayed.

Science has logical explanations for everything inside these parameters. But as consciousness expands, old explanations do not suffice, and meaning is lost; therefore, creation stories must also change. So far, our society has "gotten away with" the Big Bang Story by distracting us from the beginning miracle with dazzling scientific accomplishments: walking on the Moon; sending the Voyager spacecraft on a thirty-five-year journey to escape our solar system; decoding the human genome; expanding food production manifold using new technology; and producing an inordinate amount of consumer goods. But now that the "accomplishments" have become uncontrolled and uncontrollable, as our inventive overproduction degrades our surroundings, we are beginning to ask for more wisdom and depth in order to get a handle on our personal place in the cosmos.

A few days after graduation, my college sweetheart and I were married. I entered the adult world in the early 1970s. It was a man's world, but feminism was attempting to penetrate the nation's boardrooms and bedrooms. Independence and wealth beckoned, providing opportunities that were nonexistent just five years prior. I attended Wharton and earned an MBA in finance, finishing seventh in my graduating class. I was offered at least ten corporate jobs at the highest pay scale for new MBAs. Making my choice, I relocated across the country to California, the wealth and adventure promised land, and went to work among the men. The workplace women were all secretaries; not one held an executive position.

Several years passed. They liked my work; I was praised and promoted. It was not easy to make new friends in the big city. A vague uneasiness began to creep in. To compensate, I drank a few beers almost every night after work. In the office I had learned the ropes—financial tricks, how to bury the not-so-good results in hard-to-find places, even how to fire long-term employees when the cycle turned down. The corporate brass liked me. I was sharp.

They invited me to their martini lunches. I bought a nice house; by now, four years had passed. I was as unskilled in intimate communication as my young wife. The troops returned from Vietnam. President Nixon lied his way to near-impeachment, then resigned. Somewhere between flower children and free love, my marriage failed. The corporate work became strange. I had several new "relationships" that ended badly. Vague unrest began to haunt me more frequently now.

In line for a high management position, I had achieved my career goals early. I was a success, but in just a few years, youthful enthusiasm had vanished. The work became meaningless, the days repetitive. At night I was entertained with alcohol and old friends. Later, even those pleasures began to fade. Little was left other than day after day at the office and a growing paycheck.

Lying awake at 4:00 a.m., a thought floated up: "The world keeps letting me down; there must be more to life than this routine." The Moon beamed into my bedroom. A disembodied voice replied, "Perhaps it has been your expectations for yourself—the path you have chosen—that has let you down. The world cannot let you down. The world is the world. Only you can let yourself down. Be like the world. Be the world. Enter into her rhythms, her life. There you will be challenged, yet you will not be let down." In the morning, I gathered my courage, marched into the front office, and threw my future to the wind. I had become a corporate refugee. Alone in the world, my life purpose, my journey, had finally begun.

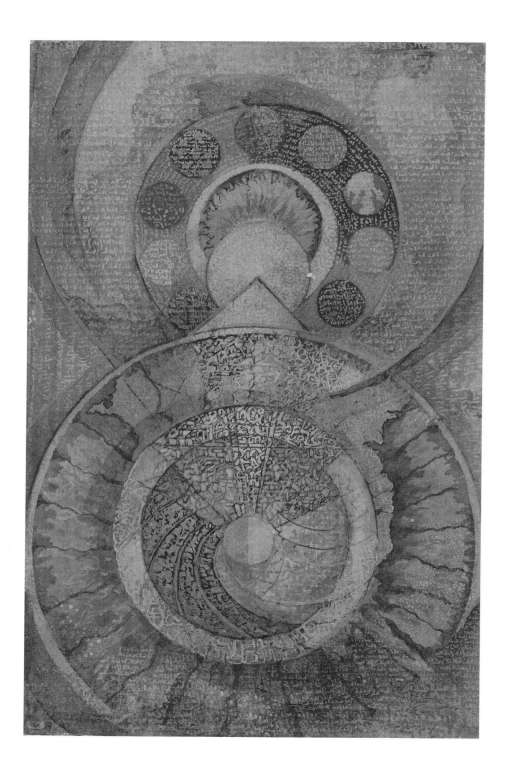

CHAPTER 6

FROM HOMINIDS TO HOMO SAPIENS

You can't call a forest a resource. It's filled with amazing
beings. You can't call the ocean, with all those fish and
marine mammals a resource. Each of these species is the end
result of 13 billion years of evolution. They're spectacular,
they're stupendous, and they have a right to be here.

—Brian Swimme

Mammals Beget Primates

Our story continues to unfold, relating recent scientific discoveries. The earliest known mammals were *morganucodontids* that lived about

210 million years ago, during the dinosaurs' reign. They were the size of today's smallest field mice, and would have fit neatly into a tablespoon. For the 145 million years following this modest beginning, dinosaur dominance dictated that mammals would remain small and inconspicuous; larger forms would be easy prey for these rapacious reptiles. By the time dinosaurs went extinct from a massive meteorite collision that caused planetwide repercussions about sixty-five million years ago, mammals had grown from mouse sized to cat sized. Their small size most likely helped mammals to survive this "K-T extinction," as it is called. It certainly provided the opportunity to gain habitat for species expansion and further growth.

The dinosaur period allowed only limited mammal diversity and size; however, by a few million years after dinosaurs disappeared, mammals had exploited the opening and multiplied prodigiously, both in variety and size. Would we humans be here today were it not for that meteorite collision? No, we would not be, not now, not in this evolutionary form. Although today's major mammal groupings began to branch from their common ancestors about one hundred million years ago, the period from sixty-five million years ago onward is called the Cenozoic Era; it is the "age of mammals." What evolutionary innovations helped us along?

Mammals are warm-blooded; we lactate to feed our young; we have hinged jaws whose configuration allows for more developed ear bones and better hearing. We have "chewing" teeth that allow more nutrients and calories to be absorbed from our foods; more calories provide additional energy to fuel a growing brain size. Marsupials are a more ancient mammalian form; placental mammals split off from a common marsupial ancestor perhaps 175 million years ago. Fifty million years of proto-Placentia forms eventually yielded *Eomaia scansoria*, "dawn mother" in Greek, as an early "mostly placental" climbing mammal living 125 million years ago. In our story, in our effort to know our place in time and space, it's enlightening to meet our early mammal mother—to "get" the connection that illuminates our common warm-bloodedness.

The Eocene geologic epoch began about fifty-five million years ago; at its beginning mammals were, for the most part, no bigger than a modern-day pig. A rapid temperature increase marked the Eocene epoch. Forestland appeared in profusion across the globe during the following few million years, extending all the way to the Polar Regions. Changing habitats provided new niches for mammals to exploit, which they did with abandon. A new order of mammalian life began to prosper: primates.

About fifty million years ago, "higher primates" developed and branched off. They were called anthropoids and were the precursors to monkeys, apes, and humans. Over the following many million years, favorable conditions in Africa allowed multiple ape varieties to develop and flourish. Today's oldest living primates are the lemur branch. An individual lemur could fit into the palm of your hand. They currently survive only in Madagascar. We humans are anthropoid's most recent branch.[9] In our Creation Story:

---

9 According to Duke University scientist Elwyn Simons about 34 million years ago a more advanced monkey developed, called *Catopithecus*. His team has uncovered fossils from the Faiyum Depression in Africa. They have the same arrangement of teeth that humans have today, leading Simons to claim: "This is the first chapter of human history."

Seventy million years ago, during the dinosaurs' rule, our mammal ancestors were small and typically nocturnal, needing to hunt at night to survive those voracious predators. With dinosaurs gone, daylight beckoned; we moved out of the night under the protection of the semidark forest, taking unprecedented risks to secure more diverse food sources. We stood on two legs, exposing our soft bellies. In the savanna we scavenged leftovers from carnivore kills, retreating to forests for safety. Eons passed. Upon discovering tools, weapons, and campfires, the old ways receded into the deep past. Caves, spears, and nighttime fires became our after-dark protectors. Predator mammals shared our habitat; we had become predators and prey alike. Larger, faster, fiercer animals predominated at night. Over many thousand generations, we moderns became unfamiliar with night's dark world; what one does not know, one tends to fear.

Hominids Separate from Primates

Humans' last common ancestor with gorillas lived about ten million years ago and with chimpanzees about seven million years ago. Our pre-human (that is, hominid) ancestors continued to branch. About four million years ago the climate began to change dramatically. It became colder; precipitation amounts and locations changed. Prior to this climate reconfiguration, hominids had expanded their African habitat; however, the new climate shrank their habitat back to the initial locations, resulting in geographic isolation near Africa's equatorial zone.

About 2.5 million years ago, the formation of Panama's isthmus created a barrier between the Atlantic and Pacific Oceans, resulting in the northern flowing Gulf Stream ocean current. This created additional climate change and was partially responsible for a series of twenty or more "ice ages," the last ending just thirteen thousand years ago. Ice ages create *big* mammals because bigger bodies are better adapted to cold weather— they retain more heat. Natural selection favored these larger animals; some became five times as large as their present-day surviving relatives. Other variables encouraged larger bodies, even in temperate zones like Australia. Both predator and prey became huge. Between one hundred thousand and twenty thousand years ago, most of this "megafauna" disappeared. By eleven thousand years ago—coinciding with humans' more sophisticated hunting skills and larger populations—all the large ice-age mammals were gone. There is an active debate in the paleontology community about whether humans are responsible for these extinctions.

What variables led to our branching away from other primates and starting, almost seven million years ago, this journey toward *Homo sapiens*, us modern humans? There are many theories, including our New Creation Story.

Our ape-like ancestors lived in the forest and spent time climbing in the trees, as do today's apes. Grasslands began to displace forests in at least one large region containing these prehominid populations; instead of continuous forests, various forest areas were separated from one another by these new grasslands. To pursue food and mating, among other activities, it benefited individuals to traverse the grasslands to get to the next forest, thereby extending their range, enabling them to obtain more food, and enhancing their possibilities to procreate. Individuals who were better at walking upright (bipedalism) had an advantage in negotiating the grasslands. They were better at finding new sources of food in these areas and at spotting predators. They gained an evolutionary advantage, survived longer, and had more offspring with similar characteristics. Eventually they became adept at living in the grasslands instead of just passing through them to the next forest. Their ape relatives remained behind in the trees. The expanding grassland ecology is, therefore, a critical participant in our evolution; perhaps it is one reason for our very existence.

Bipedalism freed up arms and hands to carry tools and weapons, transport children and supplies, manipulate stones and find new tools, more readily gather and carry food, and use bones and sticks for digging. *Australopithecus afarensis* (*A. afarensis*) was bipedal, as were all subsequent hominids, including *A. africanus.* They ate vegetables, fruits, leaves, and grass primarily. Perhaps they also scavenged meat. They did not manufacture tools but likely used tools, perhaps employing sophisticated uses. They did not hunt and did not use fire. Our story continues:

As various hominid species appeared, those with larger brains had an evolutionary advantage, especially in conjunction with tool use, controlled fire, and more refined language, which facilitated communication. Consequently, new human social configurations and interactions were made possible. Bigger brains enabled various hominid species to evolve and develop more advanced societies. It was a reinforcing cycle: controlled fire use, better tools, and more refined language stimulated brain use and gave a reproductive advantage to those individuals with larger brains. The evolution of one hominid species into another led to cultural advances, and these changes—language use, for example—evolved even larger brains.

Our Hominid Ancestors

The term *hominids* is a version of the more scientific term *Hominidae*, the family of erect, bipedal mammals, representing the taxonomic family of "great apes," which has four living genera: humans, gorillas, orangutans, and chimpanzees (bonobos are a fifth genera, if considered to be separate from chimps). *Hominids* has been used in a more specific way, that is, to describe only pre-human branches of the *Hominidae* family. These hominid branches appeared after the separation from their common ancestor with other primates. Our more recent relatives, from about two million years ago, have scientific names prefaced with "*Homo*," such as *Homo ergaster* (*H. ergaster*) and *Homo habilis* (*H. habilis*), and are referred to as "humans."

When discussing human evolution, the term "hominid" refers to various related groups (genuses) that branched off from our common primate relatives and existed prior to the genus *Homo*. As mentioned above, the term *human* refers to the genus *Homo* that evolved from hominid groups existing in earlier periods. The *Homo* genus appeared about 2.3 million years ago; we modern humans, *Homo sapiens*, are just two hundred thousand years old.

The hominid *Australopithecines* (Lucy is the celebrity) existed in the earlier periods, prior to *Homo*'s evolution. Recent fossil finds have identified up to fifteen different *Homo* species; this total is likely to increase based on the latest DNA research. Extinct *Homo* lines include our recent relatives, *H. erectus* and *H. sapiens neanderthalensis*. "Archaic *H. sapiens*" appeared perhaps four hundred thousand years ago, immediately preceding *H. sapiens* (meaning anatomically modern humans), who emerged two hundred thousand years ago.

The record of human lineage in Africa extends back more than six million years. Ethiopia alone has produced fossils of the three major phases in hominid evolution:

First, *Ardipithecus* goes back to six million years ago and existed up to about four million years ago. Found in East Africa only, these individuals used four limbs to climb in trees and were also bipedal on the ground. *Ardipithecus* lived in the woodlands and ate anything he could find that was edible—an omnivore. The hominid species called *Ar. ramidus* is an example from 4.4 million years ago.

Second, *Australopithecus* goes back to 4.2 million years ago, lasting for a remarkable 3 million years until 1.2 million years ago. Long-striding bipedalism, large chewing teeth, and dispersal throughout all Africa characterized this hominid group. The most famous example is Lucy, a 3.2-million-year-old female child. *A. afarensis* is a species that survived for perhaps six hundred thousand years; other examples are the earlier *Au. anamensis* and the later *Au. garhi*. *Australopithecus* developed the earliest stone tools 2.6 million years ago and overlapped the first of our *Homo* lineage from about 2.3 million years ago until disappearing about 1.2 million years ago.

Third, the *Homo* phase began about 2.3 million years ago in southern and eastern Africa with *H. gautengensis*, then *H. habilis* (meaning "handy man"), and a little later *H. erectus* (meaning "erect man"), who cohabited in Africa and overlapped with various earlier *Australopithecus* hominids for almost one million years. The *Homo* phase developed large brains, had smaller teeth and jaws, and used tools extensively. *H. erectus* developed Acheulean stone tools—big, symmetrical hand axes were typical. They were first to leave Africa and populate Europe and Asia.

About two million years ago, there were at least ten different hominid types alive together in Africa. As late as one hundred thousand years ago, there were at least three other *Homo* species sharing the continent with *Homo sapiens*, including *H. neanderthalsis*, *H. rhodesiensis*, *H. floresiensis*, and perhaps *H. erectus*.

There are currently more than twelve different *Homo* species as determined from fossil records and DNA research. The earliest (oldest) is called *H. gautengensis* and is a newly classified *Homo* species. According to recent work by anthropologist Dr. Darren Curnoe, "*H. gautengensis* arose more than two million years ago and survived for perhaps 1.4 million years before dying out. If so, it is older than *H. habilis*, until now thought to be the oldest *Homo* species." More hominid species are sure to be located. Our detection technology is improving: more DNA evidence is being found, new fossils are surfacing, and existing fossils in research vaults are being analyzed with more sophisticated techniques.

Dr. Curnoe describes *H. gautengensis* as having large teeth, suitable for chewing plants, and a relatively small brain. They possessed stone tools and may have been able to control fire. Individuals were only about three feet tall, weighing perhaps 110 pounds. They spent time in trees for safety and feeding; most likely they did not have language. The interesting thing about this recent determination is that new scientific research is constantly pushing human origins backward in deep time.[10]

The more recent *Homo* line includes *H. habilis* and *H. erectus* (*H. ergaster* may be the earliest *H. erectus*), each with similar attributes: they controlled fire, thereby improving their diet; they were accomplished hunters and able to kill megafauna; they learned to find and eat shellfish in addition to catching fish; and they used fire-hardened wood spears for hunting and tools. They developed Acheulean tools: hand axes with dual faces that were more elaborate and efficient for cutting and digging than the earlier epoch's Oldowan tools. This more recent Acheulean technology created smaller, sharper stone "flakes" for cutting and scraping.

---

10   A May 2010 analysis of a partial skull found decades earlier in South Africa's Sterkfontein Caves near Johannesburg identified the species, named *Homo gautengensis* by anthropologist Dr. Darren Curnoe of the UNSW School of Biological, Earth and Environmental Sciences. See Darren Curnoe, "A review of early *Homo* in southern Africa focusing on cranial, mandibular and dental remains, with the description of a new species (*Homo gautengensis* sp. nov.)," *Journal of Comparative Human Biology* (2010). doi:10.1016/j.jchb.2010.04.002.

H. erectus had a more elaborate social life, with campsites with separate areas for preparing food, cooking, getting ready for the hunt, and tool making. They may have organized into family groups around campsites; there were base camps, temporary hunting camps, and resource "gathering areas" for fruits and nuts that would be revisited in the appropriate season. *H. erectus* used red ochre (iron oxide, whose color comes from oxidation) for paint and body adornment. This group survived more than one million years; it was the first species to impact the environment by using fire and hunting—possibly hunting some large animal species to extinction.

Our progression from our ape relatives to *Homo sapiens* is complex and not fully determined. In recent decades it has been assumed that we are directly descended from *H. erectus* and before that from *H. habilis*. Scientists are now contemplating new possibilities that show a much more complex heritage. *H. erectus* may be connected to *H. sapiens* via a common ancestor, *H. ergaster*, and may have died out without evolving into *H. sapiens* as previously assumed.

A later hominid from this same lineage, *H. heildelbergenis*, may be the common ancestor of *H. sapiens* and *H. neanderthalensis*—our Neanderthal cousins with whom we shared European territory for ten thousand years prior to their going extinct. As mentioned, about two million years ago, a variety of different hominids roamed the world at the same time. Populations were small—intermingling, or even intermittent encounters between the groups, would have been rare.

The future is sure to turn up more fossils and additional DNA evidence that will clarify the missing puzzle pieces and probably determine our precise lineage from our primate beginnings to the present. All the other hominids met dead-ends. These species' existence typically ranged from between two hundred thousand and eight hundred thousand years; for example, *H. erectus* existed for about eight hundred thousand years. We can leave this family tree "sorting out" to evolutionary anthropologists, the experts in that field. (For information regarding earlier relatives that went extinct, see Appendix 5.)

Paleoneurology promises to provide more answers also; for example, about 2.5 million years ago, *Au. africanus* developed a reorganized frontal lobe in their brains, expanding the area that is responsible for planning and decision making, possibly a deciding factor in extending this species longevity to more than five hundred thousand years. In about the same era, *H. habilis*, became the first hominid with a brain size that exceeded that of a chimpanzee and was the first to make sharp-edged stone tools—a huge breakthrough. All the hominid lines first evolved in Africa.

H. erectus was the first to venture out of Africa about 1.8 million years ago. Others came later and populated a large portion of Europe and Asia before modern humans left Africa about sixty or seventy thousand years ago, eventually displacing all those who had preceded them, although there was some interbreeding. *H. erectus* had a brain size similar to that of their earlier relatives, but it was more differentiated, containing two sides—somewhat like our modern brains. This brain had more specialized cognition. They were probably the first to "tame" and use fire, although their tools were similar to those of *H. habilis*. By about six hundred thousand years ago, everyone had a big brain; and by two hundred thousand years ago, our African foreparents looked similar to today's African people; we had become anatomically modern.

We are still learning about our ancient relatives and our evolutionary development. Which hominids were in our direct lineage, and which were dead-ends? We use the current scientific research for our creation story:

Our ancient ancestors parted company with other primates about seven million years ago. That is the point when we branched from the common ancestor that we share with our closest cousins, chimpanzees, bonobos, and great apes. Our prehuman ancestors arose in Africa and migrated out to the rest of the world in various early epochs. H. erectus was first to develop the necessary skills to succeed at long migrations, leaving Africa perhaps as early as two million years ago. The next wave to leave Africa included the ancestors of Neanderthals and some other "cousin" branches to Neanderthals and modern humans, including the recently studied "Denisovans"; their ancestors began leaving Africa about eight hundred thousand years ago. They likely interbred with the earlier H. erectus populations living in Europe and other locations.

This migration was six hundred thousand years before modern H. sapiens evolved in east Africa. Between one hundred and one hundred forty thousand years after making their appearance, modern humans made their first trek out of Africa, perhaps somewhere between eighty thousand and sixty thousand years ago. Current genetic research indicates that there was some, though not extensive, interbreeding between the human newcomers and the established Denisovans and Neanderthals prior to these groups disappearing about thirty thousand years ago. Current scientific theories are evenly divided about whether or not modern humans had a hand in Neanderthals' disappearance. We seven billion moderns are the multigenetic mix produced from this intermingling.

The May 2013 *Scientific American* article "Human Hybrids" describes genetic research showing that non-Africans have about 4 percent Neanderthal genes, and some Western Pacific people have up to a 6 percent Denisovan contribution in their genome; therefore, it is evident that interbreeding did occur. It was limited in time and place, but according to this research there were human branches that went extinct, yet contributed their DNA to our modern human genome. This means that our roots include more than the single population that originally migrated from Africa. More of this fascinating mystery will be revealed from DNA research in coming years.

Geneticists tell us that various genes appear in the human genome at precise chronological junctures. As we continue to understand a particular gene's influences and determine when it appeared, we can sometimes extrapolate a cause and effect. Certain genes catalyzed advances in evolution; for example, the FOXP2 gene has a role in speech and language and appeared perhaps two hundred thousand years ago. Was this gene responsible for better communication, allowing modern humans to thrive and succeed better than, say, their contemporary Neanderthals? Maybe yes, maybe no, but this type of detective work will surely provide more answers in the future. For our story's purposes, *H. sapiens'* precise lineage is not too important. All these pre–*H. sapiens* are our relatives with almost the same DNA as ours. Minor changes in brain size and function created Earth-creature experiments with multiple variations.

Glaciation and Regeneration

The most recent (present) ice age, called the "Quaternary ice age" or "Pleistocene glaciation," began 2.58 million years ago and continues into the present, with ongoing glaciations in Antarctica. During this time period, there have been cycles of between forty-one thousand and one hundred thousand years in which ice sheets moved from the poles toward the equator, then retreated. This process changed topography by gouging out lakes and creating new river systems, raising and lowering sea levels, creating massive erosion, and redistributing mineral deposits. Ice sheets also reflect sunlight, which reduces solar absorption and further cools the climate. There have been eight glacial cycles during the past 740,000 years, as measured by modern ice core analysis.

From 2.5 million years ago to 126,000 years ago, mammals and other life-forms continued to proliferate. The famous saber-toothed tiger, woolly mammoth, and other large animals extended their ranges, coexisting with hominids and early humans, which had evolved into a various species. Approximately two hundred thousand years ago, humans became modern in size, appearance, and brain capacity. We became cleverer. It is probably not a coincidence that, in areas occupied by humans, many of the large ice age mammals disappeared during time periods that correspond with *Homo sapiens'* more efficient weaponry and advanced hunting skills. At this stage, so long ago, we had already begun to affect our environment in significant ways.

Early Homo sapiens faced and survived various natural extinction threats. There is currently an ongoing study of a volcanic eruption, one of the largest known, at Lake Toba, Indonesia, that occurred about seventy-five thousand years ago. At the time, modern humans were increasing in number and expanding their African habitat. It is theorized that this "supervolcano" ejected enough debris into the atmosphere to create a "volcanic winter," during which greatly reduced sunlight resulted in lower temperatures, killing most annual plant life. This situation may have endured for seven to ten years. There are varying estimates regarding that epoch's human population, but many researchers theorize that our species lost 60 to 75 percent of its members, with only perhaps ten thousand remaining, resulting in a "bottleneck" in human population growth. (Perhaps this event, recorded in our cellular memory, was the inspiration for the Old Testament story of Noah's Ark.)

Populations recovered; forty-five thousand years passed until the last maximum glaciation, which occurred thirty thousand years ago. When it receded about thirteen thousand years ago, the major ice sheets retreated to their current locations nearer the poles. Warming climates opened the way for the Neolithic period that followed, during which humans settled into villages and invented agriculture.

A first-generation star creates our planet's elements; it explodes into space; its remnants form our Sun and our Earth. Early in its life, Earth invents the chlorophyll molecule, enabling photosynthesis; the Sun's energy can then be embodied into new life that, after billions of years, becomes human. Self-reflective human consciousness begins copartnering in the life-giving and life-taking Earth processes.

Life is Universe-generated, emerging from a cosmic process, which Earth enables and supports. Natural Harmony is elegant relatedness. How will we learn to make wise choices as we intervene in this sacred unfolding? In the Paleolithic, indigenous, and early civilization periods, people were forced to find balance with nature to survive. It was a trial and error process; those who learned to integrate human activities with their immediate surroundings often prospered.

Later civilizations became more self-sufficient and less dependent on balancing their activities with their ecology; however, this prescientific period had a low population density, limited technical knowledge, and, therefore, a relatively low impact on the Earth. There was no urgency to focus in on the interactive, delicate balance. Things changed; we now add a billion people each twelve or thirteen years, and we see the Earth's elements as "resources" to be pillaged. Scientific evidence and coming climate chaos reflect back to us our ongoing destructive behavior.

As recently as my birth in 1945, there were only 2.5 billion people, compared to more than 7 billion humans now. We were unaware that the course we were sailing would lead to planetary havoc. Almost no one thought about it, or talked about it, or wrote about it. It was not until 1962 that Rachael Carson's *Silent Spring* brought some basic environmental issues to the public's attention. So our modern societies' involvement with

Natural Harmony is new. How might we individually reorient to realign our personal compass?

Here is a short story about how Earth processes unfold naturally. I live in Malibu, California. A nearby neighbor lived in a house on a cliff, overlooking the ocean, with about two acres of land. Like most of the homes in the area, he had planted a large variety of attractive trees, flowering plants, and grasses. Since we are in a low rainfall area, about thirteen inches per year, an irrigation system was required to keep his "garden" alive in the hot summer season and the low-rainfall spring and autumn months. Our area experienced geologic instability—land movement along the cliff area that included this property. The waterlines broke from the movement. He moved away to another home. Without water and attention, the garden slowly died and, over a few years, disappeared entirely. Even twenty and thirty-foot-tall trees withered away.

Over the next few years, I visited the property once in a while as I passed by on my daily run. Several years after its abandonment, I was able to purchase the house. With no one intervening in the abandoned garden, a transformation was occurring. After the nonnative plants, the "exotics," died off, new and different plants began to appear—native plants, trees, the indigenous spring flowers, and grasses. At first they appeared as seedlings, but in a few years there was an entirely new landscape, a native garden that required no artificial watering because it was "smart" enough to utilize the dynamic systems that the Earth provided—and, unlike expensive water from the utility company, it was all free of charge. When the artificial conditions changed to natural conditions, the exotics disappeared and made space for the native plants that are sustainable without imported water. They need almost no "gardening."

All I did over the ensuing years was to watch for the hardiest natives and encourage their propagation by removing some competition and providing more breathing room. I learned quite a lot by just watching. As water is scarce in Southern California, my new native garden is much more sustainable for my local watershed, and my water bill is one-tenth that of my neighbor. The story is meant to show that "going with the natural flow" is much easier and more cost-effective than imposing one's will on the Earth.

The lesson applies to industry also. It is possible to create products by imitating Nature instead of imposing upon Nature. As we have discussed, the Earth has created innumerable symbiotic interconnections that have developed over millions of years. Everything is recycled; there is no waste. An industrial parallel is the requirement, in some European societies, to recycle the carcasses of large appliances, like washing machines, so no new resources are needed in renewing the appliance. In another example, when we stop using fossil fuels and reorganize the auto industry, using primarily electric motors and providing public transportation in cities, we will soon reap a tremendous benefit from eliminating this current antiquated automobile era—huge asphalt-covered areas in cities will be converted to "people places," parks and gardens, all in cooperation with the living Earth. The ground below our streets and parking lots will once again become exposed to sunlight after one hundred years of nonnative, nonnatural, "exotic" uses.

Perhaps a more important analogy applies to each of us as individuals. What are the nonnative "exotics" that our parents and our culture have planted in our personal psychic and emotional makeups? It may be possible to discern their influences on our actions: the emotional drive to acquire more and more "stuff," shopping for the sake of shopping, and accumulating material possessions to the point of believing that this is a meaningful activity for our short life's "hour upon the stage."

I often ask myself, "What are my own values, my motivations? Which behaviors are at odds with Earth's rhythms?" We frequently act from artificial, culturally imposed motives, yet we each contain the elegant, interrelational wisdom that created all life on Earth. The earlier story about the abandoned garden is useful in answering the question posed above: look for the nonnatural exotics in your own emotional, psychological, and mental makeup. Don't water them; let them wither and die, thereby leaving a transformed garden within your own psyche. Our culture has built barriers, separating us from Earth's wisdom. Our worldview is often contrived, our behavior uninformed, and, consequently, we have made our surroundings toxic. By dismantling the barriers that limit wisdom, we are able to build a personal connection to Natural Harmony.

For better or for worse, humans are now co-creating life on Earth. Life's entire community has labored to birth self-reflective human consciousness. It is now important that we stand up for the rabbits, the elephants, and the slime mold. Why? To further integrate with the inexorable unknown—the "subtle wonder within mysterious darkness" that is manifesting life on Earth. If we fail, another animal will eventually pick up our torch and illuminate deeper consciousness. This creation story's journey through 3.8 billion life-years demonstrates that a lot can happen in twenty or thirty million years—many new, intelligent life forms will spring into existence. They always have.

Everything has come to pass as it needed to happen for life to arrive at this particular moment. The heart of this creation story is deepened perception—seeing one's responsibility to the planet. There is no good or bad in the story, no right or wrong, just increasing fascination. Life contains so much creative ingenuity! And now we humans have begun to co-create the planet's biology.

As we see from the extinction discussion above and in Appendix 4, there are creative cycles and destructive cycles; however, the Earth has an ongoing propensity to create more complex organisms. We have become participants in this planetary process and are now co-creation partners. Can we modify our planet and still retain a healthy ecology, as Nature does? There is almost no current evidence that we can. If the answer is no, Earth is likely retake the reins and move in a new direction. Earth is the creator and the destroyer. When the grim reaper has run its course, the empty niches created from today's extinction spasm shall be refilled. We humans are in danger of being relegated to the fossil records.

Predator or Prey

The impression we have about human evolution is that we were hunters, which required us to hone our thinking, planning, and cooperation with our fellow hunters in order to "bring home the meat." However, there is another chapter in our creation story—it is based on the epochs before we were sufficiently skilled and armed to kill saber-toothed tigers, woolly mammoths, and other megafauna that were eventually hunted to extinction. Although we developed sharp-edged tools around 2.6 million years ago, for long periods before and after inventing these new implements, our foreparents were the prey, not the predator.

Our earliest human mental and emotional development was based not on aggressive predator warrior skills but on the cunning and social "togetherness" that a "prey-species" needs to protect and feed its young. In these early times, we were more scavengers than hunters. Wits were needed, and therefore developed, to hide and escape, to fend off predators and keep the children safe.

This is the most ancient saga of our human creation story, not the hunter and warrior archetype that has evolved more recently. Remember, we always know more about recent times than about the distant past, so it is easy to make inaccurate assumptions about where we came from, especially when looking many hundreds of thousands of years into the deep past. How different a deer is from a mountain lion. Take a few minutes to visualize grass-eating animals and how they differ from meat-eating ones: their appearance; their movements; their "personalities"—all very different. Who are we humans? What is the heritage that made us what we are? That is the question we are sorting through in these pages. Anthropology and our DNA show that we are not just the aggressive, warmongering people of recent history.

The year was 1982. I was in my midthirties, seeking adventure, looking for meaning and exploring exotic places. I was attempting to get into Tibet. This was difficult to do because, for political reasons, the Chinese had closed Tibet to outsiders; however, eventually I was able to talk my way into a short-term visa and go across the border. The Tibetan plateau, at twelve thousand feet, was a most unusual place: stark, level grass-land prairie expanses crisscrossed with alpine streams; few trees; almost no vegetables; omnipresent Sun beating down; frequent winds; yak herders; and Buddhist temples. But the thing that impressed me the most was the trip down the moun-tain into Nepal. Halfway down, the treeless, rocky, snake-like road tunneled into a lush rainforest with rushing waterfalls, tropical ferns, and thick vines hanging from towering broad-leafed trees. In this place where no one goes, I sat still under an arching willow branch with verdant grasses everywhere. There was a gurgling stream flowing below me. I lifted my head and spoke aloud so the circling birds could hear me: "Why is it so beautiful in this remote place, and so often not beautiful in the city?" Leaning back against the trunk in con-templation, an answer came in response: "We exist through the grace of the living Earth's embrace. Like all the other animals, we are dependent for our survival upon our Earth's healthy functioning." I recognized the voice—my dream companion, Sophia—and her invitation to summon her for insights about "survival issues." So I asked her, "Why, in this peaceful place, do I have a premonition that something terrible is happen-ing out in the densely peopled human world?" Sophia's voice again rode in on the breeze: "You are in a complex situation. Everyday activities, travel, entertainment, and food choices are literally changing the atmosphere's composition. You are caught in a potentially suicidal cycle that can only be changed by a shift in people's awareness—otherwise you will destroy your own life support system." I'd heard enough. My mind became empty. The breeze became still; the falling water and bird songs were the sole remaining soul sounds.

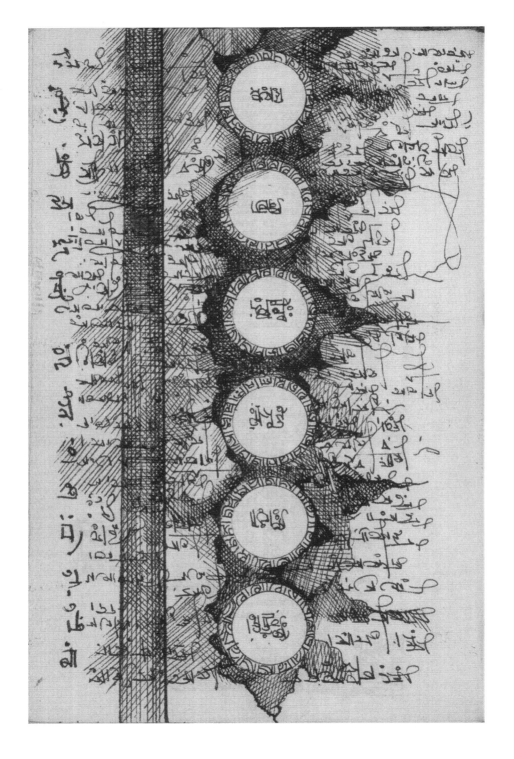

CHAPTER 7

TOOLS, FIRE AND LANGUAGE

The premodern world had been permeated with spiritual,
mythic, theistic and other humanly meaningful categories,
but all of these were regarded by the modern perception
as anthropomorphic projections. Mind and matter, psyche
and world were separate realities. The scientific liberation
from theological dogma and animistic superstitions was thus
accompanied by a new sense of human alienation from a
world that no longer responded to human values nor offered
a redeeming context within which could be understood the
larger issues of human existence.

—Rick Tarnas

As science delves deeper into human beginnings, and the more fossils and DNA evidence we examine, the further back in time our origins are revealed to be. This is also the case when looking at the scientific research about the first use of fire, sophisticated language, and improved technology for making tools—all critical steps in our emergence from smart apes to self-reflecting philosophers.

Tools

Although animals often use tools, no nonhominid animal, including any primate, has been known to hit one stone against another with the purpose of creating a sharp-edged tool. The oldest known manufactured stone tools date from 2.6 million years ago; they are called Oldowan tools, named after the Olduvai Gorge where they were first discovered, which is a ravine in Africa's eastern Serengeti Plains, located in present-day Tanzania. Troves of similar tools have been discovered in east Africa dating to 1.8 million years ago, which indicates that stone toolmaking technology did not change during almost a million-year period.

Before stone tools were manufactured, it is likely that large stones called "manuports" were transported from site to site and used to break scavenged bones and procure the nutritious marrow inside. It is important to keep in mind that there is a distinction between using "found" tools and actually manufacturing tools for use. Naturally, the former predated the latter. Until recently, we believed that early hominids first used tools about 2.6 million years ago. This was a few hundred thousand years before the extensive use of tools by *H. habilis*, reaching back more than two million years.

The most recent evidence of the first tool use places this activity almost a million years earlier, with *Au. afarensis*, the species that produced Lucy. The journal *Nature* cites evidence from cut marks on bones that these hominids were butchering meat with stone tools and breaking the bones for the nutritious marrow as early as 3.4 million years ago. (Lucy has been dated to 3.2 million years ago. For more information see Appendix 6.)

As mentioned, simply using tools is not evidence of manufacturing tools. Finding sharp-edged stones and using them to butcher meat is a big advancement, but making tools purposefully is another level of accomplishment. By utilizing tools, food varieties could be expanded, and meat was added to the diet. Without tools, nuts, fruits, flowers, and tender shoots were the primary foods; the addition of stone tools also allowed plants to be ground and processed so that a wider range of choices became available. This era exhibits the earliest evidence that our ancient ancestors consumed meat, which provided significantly more energy to develop and maintain increased brain size. Human brains use about 20 percent of all the body's energy, and compact nutrition in the form of meat can more readily provide this high-energy requirement.

H. gautengensis, from 2.3 million years ago is the most ancient *Homo* species known. Tool manufacture appears to predate the genus *Homo* by only a few hundred thousand years. Our creation story:

The proximity in time of tool manufacture and genus Homo *emerging is important, creating the possibility that this toolmaking practice and the expanded nutrition it provided were critical in the transformation of more archaic hominids into the Homo lineage that has become modern humans. These stone tools fundamentally altered hominids' association with their environment. From the standpoint of worldview and attitude, during this transition period, our foreparents changed from prey to scavenger and eventually to a hunting predator. As we transitioned from vegetarian to carnivore, new species arose apace.*

As mentioned, the first manufactured tools, Oldowan, were made by hominids about 2.6 million years ago. This period is referred to as the "Basel Paleolithic." Manufactured from stones that could fit in a small hand, they were made by striking one stone with another in a precise way to produce a cleaved side, tapering to a cutting edge. Striking the opposite side produced two cleaved sides, with a sharp edge at the bottom. Not all stones were suitable for the "striker" stone or for the tool implement being made; therefore, planning ahead and learning about various stone types and their characteristics was essential. This required knowledge of crystal-line rock characteristics; for example, how to strike them on a particular plane to create chopping, hammering, digging, and cutting implements: striking the core stone with a hammer stone, in the correct manner, yields sharp edges for chopping or cutting. This knowledge was passed from generation to generation.

Hominids were using found tools 3.4 million years ago. There is an eight-hundred-thousand-year transition period before Oldowan tools are manufactured. Oldowan tools are the first sophisticated manufactured tools. As our story has suggested, the proximity of this time frame to the emergence of the genus *Homo*, our genus, is likely not a coincidence. By helping to procure meat, these tools tangentially helped *Homo's* larger brain to develop.

After more than a million years, tool design finally advanced. Acheulean stone tools were a catalyst for our evolutionary development. Much more could be accomplished with this newer technology. The resulting challenges from employing these more useful tools helped to hone the intellect over time. Acheulean tools appeared perhaps one million years ago (estimates range from 1.5 million to 700,000 years ago). What were the improvements? Visualize a rock that is perhaps eighteen inches long, three times larger than a prior Oldowan tool, that has been chipped and flaked for its entire length into a rounded handle on one end and an ax on the other.

Axes, picks, and cleavers were produced. This innovation, along with other highly processed implements, afforded many more uses—extending the capacity for processing more nutritious foods, thereby providing more fuel for larger bodies and brains. This tool inventory remained basically the same, with some refinements, for many hundred thousand years. It included knifelike cutting edges, scrapping tools, needles, axes, and more—all made from flint and other sharp-edged stones. The Acheulean tool period was a time of multiple hominids and *Homo* species, all exploring various niches with the help of fire, protolanguages, and tools. Only a few slipped through the bottleneck. All other human species had their time in the sun and then disappeared.

Acheulean technology prevailed into more recent times when two *H. sapiens* species, Cro-Magnons and *H. neanderthalensis*, began to interact in Europe, resulting in an even more functional tool inventory: knives, needles, and other blades were created from stone and bone materials. (More detailed information is provided in Appendix 7.)

Fire: First Use

Early *Homo* species went through long periods with little change. The controlled use of fire was likely one of the most important breakthroughs, along with tools and spoken language, in advancing hominids' development. Fire was critical in catalyzing human biological evolution and the evolution of human consciousness. When did humans first control fire? Was this skill a widespread phenomenon initially, or was it isolated for long periods before becoming generally available to all human populations? The paleoanthropology debate around these questions is unresolved.

There is a great deal of support for the hypothesis that controlled fire occurred with *H. erectus* earlier than 250,000 years ago. It seems likely that the widespread controlled use of fire helped *H. erectus* and other archaic humans to transition into our modern form. Scientists are finding a great deal of evidence in Europe and Asia for campsites, charcoal, flint, burnt bones, and fire-hardened wood spears from about 250,000 years ago.

In the paleontologist community, there are many claims that fire was used in earlier periods—but was it controlled use? Was it widespread or isolated? How far back does it go?

There are examples at the Cave of Hearths in South Africa, which has "burned deposits" dated from to hundred to seven hundred thousand years ago; at Qesem Cave, twelve kilometers east of Tel-Aviv, evidence exists for the fire use 382,000 years ago. Other Israeli researchers claim dates as far back as 790,000 years. At Zhoukoudian in China, evidence of fire is as early as 460,000 years ago; at Trinil, Java, blackened bone and charcoal deposits have been found among *H. erectus* fossils dated from 830,000 years ago. Multiple fire-related sites in Europe have also been associated with *H. erectus*; for example, at Torralba and Ambrona, Spain, evidence includes charcoal in association with Acheulean stone tools dated three to five hundred thousand years ago. Some scholars place the first use much earlier. The most extreme claims extend back 1.5 million years.

The first controlled fire use most likely was "captured" from wildfires. *H. erectus* was intelligent enough to protect charcoal embers and transport these precious coals from one campsite to another. Most likely this was a task assigned to one of the group's most capable and responsible members; a dying ember meant no campfire, which would endanger the entire band. Recapturing fire, although an utmost priority, might take months. Over many millennia, flint stone and, perhaps, other methods to produce fire independently replaced the "capture and carry" process.[11]

---

11 See sources: "First Control of Fire by Human Beings—How Early?" http://www.beyondveg.com/nicholson-w/hb/hb-interview2c.shtml; Gowlett,"Fire was used by Homo erectus in northern China more than 400,000 years ago, and there is sketchy evidence suggesting that it may have been used long before that (1984, pp. 181-82); David Price, "Energy and Human Evolution", James, Steven R. (Feb. 1989); "Hominid Use of Fire in the Lower and Middle Pleistocene: A Review of the Evidence," *Current Anthropology*, (University of Chicago Press). In addition, South Africa's Wonderwerk Cave shows evidence of controlled fire dating back more than 300,000 years.

As previously discussed, tool making required hitting various types of stones at certain angles to produce sharp edges. These techniques were developed from trial and error—all stones found would have been tested for suitability. Surely, flint, a sharp-edged stone, was tested as a resource for a potential tool. Tool making trials likely included many experiments involving flint. Hitting flint against flint produces sparks. Whether the tool production attempts were successful or not, sparks were a byproduct; a few of these efforts may have unintentionally ignited dry leaves that happened to be on the ground below the flint stone experiment. Voilà, "made" fire is discovered![12]

Fire not only provided warmth that would allow migration from tropical to more temperate climatic zones, it also extended productive activity into the nighttime: skinning animals, making tools, and socializing around the campfires. Fire increased the tribe's safety by warding off carnivores, reducing insect populations, and killing harmful food bacteria. Fire cooked food. Because cooked food is more readily digested, more food types became available. Better absorption into the digestive system results in better physiological body function, including more usable calories for hunting and gathering.

Over time, evolutionary advances followed controlled fire use: longer life, more offspring, and bigger brains. *H. erectus* also used fire to improve its tools and weapons; for example, fire-hardened spears allowed *H. erectus* to hunt larger animals and provide meat more often. Wood hardened in domestic fire pits was turned into harpoons for fishing. The sharp points may also have been good tools to extract meat from shellfish.

---

12 Hominids made the first tools about 2.6 million years ago. *H. erectus* created much more sophisticated tools about 1.6 million years later, one million years ago.

It is not a coincidence that extensive use of controlled fire by 250,000 years ago, combined with more sophisticated tools, was a critical factor in the transition from earlier *Homo* species into *H. sapiens* about 200,000 years ago. Large brains use vast amounts of energy compared to other bodily processes. Providing sufficient brain fuel required better protein sources and more carbohydrate sugars. This was made possible by cooking foods. Ancient man became modern man by becoming proficient with fire, tools, and language. The *H. erectus* campfires may also have been instrumental in creating the earliest family units: groupings based on mother and father cooking, eating, and sleeping together, with their children around the same fire—a big step in the evolution of social grouping.

Language

As we know, modern human anatomy was in place by two hundred thousand years ago, but culture and behavior are developed and passed on over many millennia. When did we starting acting in modern ways? New evidence will emerge from the fossil record. It will yield bones, valuable DNA, and various other artifacts. It's likely that the time frames for modern cultural activities will be pushed backward into even deeper time than currently assumed: symbolic thought; language; aesthetic qualities built into tools and weapons; elaborate burial sites and rituals; sacred objects; art for art's sake; ceremonial sites used for sacred gatherings; body adornment and jewelry; music making and sophisticated toolmaking. All this and much more defines the long transition from becoming physiologically modern to behaving in modern ways.

Did major advances in creativity blossom forty or fifty thousand years ago as has recently been taught, or did these symbolic processes evolve slowly over more than a thousand centuries, eventually producing the many artifacts that date back to forty thousand years ago? As more evidence is accumulated, we will "see" further back in time. Instead of particular watershed moments, humans' literal and abstract mental development probably made slow progress over long time periods. With the hardware in place, the skull and brain size, our ancestors branched into a great many cognitive experiments.

Some ingenious discoveries died out with their discoverers, perhaps a particularly advanced individual. Even when taught to others, advances may have disappeared when a tribal group—holders of that wisdom—died off. When human population reached a critical density and more frequent interaction occurred, "modern" behavior, such as advanced symbolic thought and abstract art, became generalized throughout the species. This is evident by about forty thousand years ago; however, some of these accomplishments surely appeared and disappeared many times in isolated areas before becoming widespread.

An abstract cave painting is a representation of symbolic thought— mental symbols manifest in literal form. A spoken noun is typically a symbol representing a particular object. A poetic line is often a verbally expressed mental concept standing for an emotion or a sacred event. Language is a "complexification" of the human condition. It started simply with lots of nouns and is continually deepening its potential to communicate more intricately. We were highly evolved intuitive creatures prior to language, as are many animals around us; however, more sophisticated language and advancing mental conceptualizations go hand in hand.

Since the earliest written languages are only about 5,000 years old, with alphabetic languages beginning just 3,500 years ago, the human mind was initially sharpened from spoken languages. It is unlikely that we could have become self-reflective without language. We could think in complex ways, as other large-brained mammals do, but without the inter- active communication that language makes possible, we could not think *about* ourselves thinking, or about where we came from and our eventual destiny. In short, the rational mind could not have developed as it has. Both intuition and rationality are needed for some of our most complex mental achievements; honing these skills is probably dependent on the give-and-take between individuals that language facilitates.

When did language arise? To create complex language, one must have the necessary physical anatomy, including the neurological brain connec- tions, and the cultural opportunity for communication. When did the *Homo* lineage develop the voice box and the lengthened pharynx that would allow the necessary intonations and inflections used in our speech patterns? No other animal, including our ape relatives, makes these sorts of sounds. Fossil evidence has traced this physiological development back to *H. heidelbergensis* in Ethiopia dating to six hundred thousand years ago; other, sketchier evidence goes back to *H. ergaster*, who lived two million years ago.

Were these voice box and pharynx changes important in Darwinian natural selection? Did they contribute to particular species' higher survival rates? Was communication critical for survival? The Neanderthal had a much more rudimentary anatomy for sophisticated communication, while developing a complex society that survived until twenty-eight thousand years ago. Indeed, there is a current debate in the anthropological community about whether or not Neanderthals could use speech in more than cursory ways; however, other communication forms—such as sign language, emotional and relational bonding, and possibly ESP—may have accentuated their interactions. These intuitive skills likely exceeded those of their *H. sapiens* contemporaries.

Language helps to develop the rational mind, and modern humans were probably more rational than their Neanderthal cousins. All the dominating, patriarchal societies arose concurrently with written languages; it's likely that the rational mind is better at domination than the intuitive mind. After us modern humans and Neanderthals coexisted for ten thousand years together in Europe, the Neanderthal went extinct. Rationality is exceptionally good at competition.

Most, if not all, animals, given the physical apparatus and the intelligence, do their best to communicate. It can be assumed that ancient *Homo* genus peoples did the same—utilized their physical capacity and intelligence to make sounds, expressions, and gestures that expressed information and emotion between one another. My personal example is my son, Leonardo. At eighteen months he was intelligent and highly aware of all that was going on around him, but he was using words much less often than his peer group—almost not at all. Then I noticed a strange phenomenon: Leo was creating his own names, that is, unique sounds for objects, including celestial ones. He was inventing his own language!

I went along for the ride and learned his names for the things he pointed to. We soon had a protolanguage going. Leo spoke in individual words, many his own invention, long after his contemporaries were using sentences. About the time we were beginning to worry about this situation, he uttered his first English language sentence: "I can do it." From then onward, Leo's protolanguage disappeared into his mind's recesses. My daughter made no effort to invent language, so I assume it's not every child's mission.

That experience leads me to theorize that the same thing has happened thousands, if not a million, times over the millennia that humans learned to talk. An individual leads the way, and his or her tribe catches on, uses the new words to communicate, then teaches them to the next generation. Perhaps, to begin this process, our ancient prehuman relatives needed at least the mental acuity of today's twenty-four-month-old child, combined with the extended pharynx. Scientists can tell us approximately when the ancient brain first became large enough. It was probably at least a few million years ago; a more precise time frame is not necessary for this story.

Suffice it to say, speech and communication most likely developed apace, when the necessary physical and mental capacity became available. As brains became larger, spoken communication became more sophisticated. By the time our brains reached their modern proportions two hundred thousand years ago, we probably had the potential for today's intricate communication; however, it took many thousands of years for the modern brain's neuron pathways to knit together in the special connections required to create communication beyond rudimentary vocabulary. Time passed; generations came and went, each making a contribution. Syntax became more complex, as did sentence structure; and, eventually, William Shakespeare arrived.

Communication versus Language

Speech is not necessarily language, and language not necessarily speech. Communication using vocal sounds is not the same as speech. Many animals can use symbolic representations to communicate, so using symbols in communication is not enough to be considered language. Macaws often live to seventy years and longer. They are extremely intelligent and can "speak" in sentences after learning vocabulary from the humans around them. They remember words and speak them at a later time; speech, yes, language, no. Kanzi is a great ape that has been trained to communicate using lexigrams, symbols that represent concepts like, "I'd like to have an apple, please"; or, "Please open the door to the other part of my enclosure." This is symbolic communication, yes; language, no.

In the wild, chimpanzees have different calls for different important events: one type of call for an approaching eagle; a different call for a poisonous snake; and, yet again, another for a youngster calling for mother. In the last instance the mother will immediately look at her offspring while other mothers look at the mother being called to, presumably to be sure she got the message. This behavior is vocal, it's communication, it's sophisticated—but, again, it cannot be called language.

Given the many eye-opening research experiments with animal communication, it seems reasonable that our ancient hominid foreparents used all the mental and physical skills at their disposal to communicate, and eventually create language. The interesting question for our Creation Story and the evolution of human consciousness is: when was this watershed skill finally integrated in a generalized way into human behavior—and to what extent did this special faculty catalyze further evolution?

What constitutes "language," and what is the most likely epoch in which hominids obtained this skill? Studying language origins is called "glottogony." Linguists have sophisticated ways to analyze language types and complexities. The first communication likely included sounds combined with gestures and emotional immediacy dependent on the message's importance. Vocabulary grew, incorporating more and more symbolic concepts, much like Kanzi's lexicon skills. At some point, that evolved into syntax and greater sophistication. Eventually, fully symbolic representations could be mentally manipulated. Abstract contemplation was born.

Many mammals with large brains exhibit complex consciousness; they are extremely intelligent and acutely aware of what's going on around them. Dolphins can recognize themselves as separate individuals in a mirror; dogs and perhaps many other animals can, also; however, we humans became the first "self-reflecting" animals, meaning we not only think using symbols and language, we also think about ourselves thinking! We contemplate the past and future. We philosophize about our origins, mortality, and morality. We imagine and create inventions from our imaginations. These attributes are not possible without language development. Sophisticated language, once available, catalyzed innovation: physical inventions, more intricate social groupings, better hunting efficiency, and higher survival rates in times of duress. Eventually we penetrated into the heavenly cosmos—the human animal left the planet and walked on the Moon.

It's possible that symbolic language emerged in conjunction with the first use of stone tools about 2.6 million years ago. Perhaps this was only a protolanguage. Some "experts" theorize that complex language arose as late as fifty thousand years ago and was responsible for driving modern behavior's emergence and proliferation: abstract art, better tools, new hunting techniques, jewelry, long-distance trading, and more; however, it is more likely that language developed gradually from the earliest physiological possibility, advancing in parallel with voice box and brain development for more than two million years. Language was the most important influence in the advance from our earliest *Homo* relative to us moderns.

There are many ways to become more intimate with the Earth: perhaps, spend some time in the forest—long enough for a wild-forest animal to come up to you—to be interested in you. Are you initially afraid of the dark forest? It might take a little time, perhaps a few visits. Allow yourself to immerse more deeply in this "forest meditation." Let your fear fade away; become open to being in intimate embrace with the forest. It may be minutes, or perhaps days, but the animals will come. When they are comfortable joining you, then you will also have become a forest-being.

Sophia

CHAPTER 8

NATURAL HARMONY

The intuitive mind is a sacred gift and the rational mind is a faithful servant. We have created a society that honors the servant and has forgotten the gift.

—Albert Einstein

Our New Creation Story has now woven its way from the Big Bang to the emergence of modern humans two hundred thousand years ago. The biological evolution portion of the story is anchored in recently discovered information derived from DNA showing that all today's living humans have a common ancestry and genesis in East Africa, with one common mother, Mitochondrial Eve, a woman estimated to have lived in Africa between one hundred fifty thousand and two hundred thousand years ago.

This common Mother is not the Bible's proverbial Eve. Mitochondrial Eve was born long after the earliest *Homo sapiens*; however, due to events like the - catastrophe, it was her lineage alone that survived.

There are credible theories describing population bottlenecks, including the Toba catastrophe, suggesting that human population declined from many hundred thousand to perhaps fifteen thousand (some estimate only two thousand) people about seventy-five thousand years ago, with this entire group confined to eastern and southern Africa. All of today's European and Asian peoples are descended from these common ancestors, who later migrated out of Africa, starting about sixty or seventy thousand years ago. These are the people who, many centuries later, populated the planet's remaining geographical locations.

Just as recently we have learned, and continue to learn, about our ancestors' ten-thousand-year interaction with our parallel *Homo sapiens*, the Neanderthals, who were living in Europe when we out-of-Africans got there. There was a ten-thousand-year time overlap before the Neanderthals' disappearance, which occurred for no obvious reason—leaving us to speculate about their decimation by our forefathers. There is current evidence also indicating some limited interbreeding with our species.

Has there ever been an epoch in modern humans' two-hundred-thousand-year history when we perceived our human condition to be one people on a shared planet, interdependent, concerned with each other's welfare, and behaving in a conscious way? Not yet. Did early human bands and tribes concern themselves with all other groups? Did the first humans to reach Europe worry about Neanderthals' continued existence? No, but perhaps the time is here. The planet demands it, our children demand it, and spiritual growth demands it. The alternatives are too dire and ugly to hand off to future generations. The new ways that humans will relate to others and to the Earth, if we make it through our current ecological bottleneck catastrophe, constitute the next step in the evolution of human consciousness.

Our new story "takes in" the Earth as a sacred entity. It is spiritual but not religious and can even enhance the world's great religious traditions without detracting from them. Although there is a budding movement within many religions, or factions thereof, toward recognizing Earth's sacredness, there is not a *demand* for environmentally responsible conduct.

Spirit is essential. Spirit connects us, provides intimacy with all things, and imbues meaning and great-full-ness. These deeper connections teach us to care. We begin to "see" the Earth's interdependent life principles. We become the "new human" through heart, love, and intimacy. All our senses are expanded, as is our compassion. Given the Earth's ongoing decimation, this opening to greater depth and concern is also bound to provoke anxiety and grief. Our emotional range is expanded, top to bottom. Grief and joy combine to make us more fully alive.

Each animal species is special in its own way: the spider spinning her silk web; the fifty-million-year-old whale species perfectly attuned to its surroundings; frolicking dolphins with exuberant sex lives; large-brained elephants, saddened by loss, returning to the place of a relative's death to grieve for their loved one. The human animal is less integrated with its surroundings but fully engaged in the planetary experiment of developing *self-reflective* consciousness. This particular type of conscious awareness— to think about thinking, to philosophize, to contemplate our origins and life after death—is, at this point in the Earth's history, unique to our species. We have embodied "Earth wisdom" in new ways and have opened our physical selves, our brains, our minds, and our cells to these revelations. We have made these philosophical concerns conscious. We talk about them.

We do not create wisdom; it exists with or without us. I'll define "wisdom" as it applies to this discussion: *valid information that is an accurate representation of what the "world" is and how it functions; in other words, the nature of reality*. We are only able to invent something, to "make" things, to the extent that we accurately tease out information that has always existed and that guides Earth's functioning. We are children of the Earth, using the barest, newly acquired scientific tidbits of Earth's wisdom to manipulate our surroundings.

The term *Universal Consciousness* can be used as a noun, representing a disembodied entity. The Earth created us, just as the Earth created a polar bear and a brightly colored macaw. Prior to humans appearing, "Earth-wisdom-consciousness" existed as it does now; however, there was "no one" to contemplate it, to discuss its idiosyncrasies. The Earth had not yet put this biointelligence in place until it created us humans. Without self-reflection, a human being's consciousness is not much different from that of the other large-brained primates, or whales, or elephants. Consciousness exists with or without humans. In this human creation story, how we interrelate with Universal Consciousness is an important plot line.

For billions of years Earth has been "inventing" things—biological things like butterflies, dinosaurs, and humans; geological things like stalagmites and volcanoes. Yes, we humans have invented automobiles and airplanes. If you take a long walk in the forest, as I often do, you will some-times find one of our ubiquitous creations, an old car for example, lying by a creek bed or down a ravine, perhaps fifty years old, rusted, decomposing, half covered in flowering vines. It is returning to the Earth. Can you imag-ine the amount of the US federal budget it would take to "invent" a robotic honeybee, or an American eagle? Maybe we're not so smart after all.

Are we going to continue as a parasite existing only by taking from the Earth, or can we become a symbiotic partner with the planet? Initially, and for more than 99 percent of our existence, we humans have been inte-grated into the larger Earth community. In recent times we have become, and continue to be, parasitic. Our species has created an unhealthy ecol-ogy for our fellow biological travelers on "spaceship Earth."

Our awareness has changed, and our behavior is beginning to change. As we integrate more and more Earth consciousness into our human consciousness, we learn how to live without harming our surroundings. We now know how to do so, but knowing and doing are different. And that is the dramatic thread of our creation story; first, becoming more conscious; next, integrating this wisdom into our collective culture; and finally, behaving differently as an entire species—acting as though other species matter; making choices so that Earth's healthy functioning takes priority over personal and national greed.

Fear and Longing on a Lonely Planet

I have begun writing a book called *Why America Fears the Dark*. Of course, it's not just Americans who are in this predicament; Europeans and many Asians are also afraid of their own shadows, as are most people in the modern world. I was born at the end of World War II; there were two and a half billion people on the planet, now we have seven billion and rising—all this increase during my lifetime. As most who were alive at my birth have now passed on, almost all seven billion are new to the planet since my birth! Catholic churches have suffered from sex scandals; religious skepticism is on the rise in America and Europe. "Scientism" has been elevated to a cultural icon, its creative ingenuity idolized on the altar of consumerism.

We are adrift in an ocean of meaninglessness. Some find solutions in religious fundamentalism, attempting to impose *their* beliefs on everyone so that they can feel confident that *their* god is *the* god and *their* afterlife, based on *their* version of heaven, is secure. In contemporary consumer societies, these fundamentalists, although vocal beyond their numbers, are a minority. Most of the remaining scientifically oriented, automobile-driving citizens have come face-to-face with existential questions and fears: Who am I? What am I doing here on Earth? Where did I come from? What will happen to me when I die?

Our society's solution is to repress this anxiety by doing what? Going shopping! This was President George W. Bush's advice to solve the recession that followed the 9/11 World Trade Center catastrophe. Sounds superficial? It's actually a thoroughly considered strategy to reduce existential fear by distracting the population with more "stuff": mass multimedia, video games, football, the latest fashion, faster cars, and shoes with blinking lights for kids—on and on.

As long as Harry Potter films and late-night talk show "entertainment" is able to distract the citizens, they will not be paying attention to the oil wars in the Middle East and human starvation in Africa. The American "way of life" is sacrosanct and justifies atrocities around the world for the purpose of gathering the resources that enable that lifestyle to survive. The United States has 5 percent of the world's population and uses 25 percent of its resources. Why are those resources so important that we are willing to go to war over them? They keep our economic engines humming to repress an entire culture's existential fear of the unknown— death and the terror of annihilation. The Catholic Church has a system to address these fears, but in the Northern Hemisphere, it has lost respect and is no longer believable to the masses. Enter consumerism, distraction, and repression. Why are we, as individuals and as a culture, so intent on hiding from death's door?

The current social structure around the planet is male dominated and patriarchal. I'll make a generality here (of course, there are many exceptions to this statement): the richest guys, with outsized egos and often aggressive, overbearing personalities full of judgment, criticism, and opinions—these are often the guys in charge. Some are truly drawn to serve the public, so hats off to them, because spending one's life making rules and budgets to control one's fellow citizens is emotionally draining work. Visionary politicians are few and far between. It's also hard to get one elected; he or she would face a grinding process in attempting to make change. However, this is our challenge—to transform our culture, including all our decisions makers: politicians, priests, army generals, educators, nutritionists, entertainers, doctors, and all the rest.

Self-preservation requires discrimination; when I look over a one-hundred-foot-high precipice, I know not to dance at the edge. Is this fear, wisdom, or perhaps a little of both? When I see video of mountain goats moving amid the ledges on treacherous cliffs, it makes my stomach queasy; I would be in grave danger in that situation, but the goats are not. If I were to somehow find myself in such a situation, my fear would debilitate me; the goat moves blithely along. If he were afraid, it would be detrimental to his safety. His skills are different than mine; he does not need to fear this height while walking on three-inch-wide ledges. Some humans climb Yosemite's Half Dome without ropes. My healthy fear keeps me on the ground; I know my limitations.

Animals know when to fear for self-preservation. A horse is a runner, like an antelope. Have you seen a horse trapped in a corral while a fire rages nearby? He demonstrates the terror of self-preservation because he can't run away; he's trapped. It's unnatural to not run; his panic worsens his predicament. The horse experiences physical life-and-death fear when trapped in the fire. This fear is in our animal nature, too; however, the goat and horse do not suffer existential fear because they do not have self-reflective consciousness, that is, they do not think about thinking or about their existence. Rather, they live in the moment and think about what is occurring around them. This ubiquitous animal thinking often includes planning ahead—a squirrel gathers nuts for the winter—but this planning is mostly biologically programmed. We humans, in our logical minds, fear the unknown; we fear the dark.

For the most part, our spiritual traditions are failing us. Spirit has been banished, and the natural desire for connection with the Divine has been repressed. Nature is seen as dangerous. Science attempts to conquer and control her unruly dynamism. Predators live in dark forests. In our current culture, Nature, the unknown, is scary, so we need to build up our security: money in the bank, several cars, big houses, and hoarding the world's natural resources. We are driven by the fear of death in our attempt to delay death. We distract ourselves with mass media in an effort to ignore death. It was not always this way.

We are at the end of a five-thousand-year period that cycled us away from connection and intimacy—the feminine values discussed earlier. This cycle is not good or bad. It is a natural process: the sacred Earth in conjunction with the universal Creative Source, evolving animal consciousness toward intimacy with the Divine. It is not a master plan; rather, an experiment. If it fails, a new unfolding will begin.

The current science-as-master epoch has outlived its usefulness. We've torn apart the whole to examine its parts; we've learned to fly to outer space and to celestial bodies; we've discovered that matter and energy are the same thing in different forms; we have witnessed matter blinking in and out of existence. But our science, and our "stuff," has become the way we perceive the world; logos reigns, and intuition is submerged.

Our new story combines Earth-honoring wisdom with scientific accomplishment for the first time. It is essential that we incorporate the latest scientific knowledge. Until recently, all modern science resided in the "dark"—that fecund, unconscious, mysterious, and feared place from which all creation arises. We have coaxed out and thrown light on many mysteries but lost sight of Earth as provider and sustainer. It is her living systems that support and nurture us all. In our adolescent masculine exuberance (a beautiful thing in children playing sports), we overstepped the mark. We have submerged and silenced the wise-elder voices, both female and male, that carry Earth's perennial wisdom.

Another Look at Stuff

One does not crave that which has not yet been invented. For example, indigenous people are often more content when they are not aware of all the modern consumer goods, or "stuff." This is also true for us city-dwelling moderns; it's hard to covet something that has not yet been invented. But if that fancy new "mobile processing device" has twelve additional "apps," then we want one! Interestingly, spiritual psychologists argue that the way to find spirit and meaning is usually *through* the stuff, not by avoidance of it. So go ahead, have the stuff, at least some of the stuff, at least a taste of the stuff, all in order to realize that "stuff" will not provide one's life with depth—only caring relationships and intimate experiences can do that.

We can't deny indigenous people, or India and China's billions, the modern world's inventions for personal entertainment and transportation. What we can do is to provide an alternative model of a better life beyond the yearning for many of these not-so-necessary things—a fuller and happier life based on meaning and depth—so that fewer people, indigenous or urban, get trapped in the meaningless distraction of money and material success. Deepened resonance with the world's relational nature gives us better balance, reducing our craving for more stuff.

Each professional discipline can be woven into our New Creation Story's fabric, defining *our* human epoch. Ecological economics, ecological medicine, ecological law, ecological education, and ecological politics—all these and many more "eco-disciplines" are coming to the fore. Put the "stuff" in its proper emotional place, then distribute it fairly among the many; then we will have a fighting chance to solve our current crisis.

Successful native societies that lived in harmony with their natural surroundings did so within their situation's particular context. Most tribal societies in place when Western culture came upon them were long social experiments in trial and error and survival. The archeological record shows that many others did not acclimate as well and subsequently disappeared, perhaps partially from not developing an integrative philosophy that could guide them in embracing their natural surroundings. The Earth-honoring indigenous wisdom that did survive is integrated into our New Creation Story.

We are in a rapid transformation catalyzed by our precarious affiliation with nature; this transition is both individual and cultural. How does social change occur? One by one, person by person, an individual's consciousness deepens; this affects his or her surroundings (friends, neighbors, town council, et cetera), spreading a deeper understanding of the nature of reality. Social change follows: tobacco smoking becomes a public health issue; the Berlin Wall falls; nonpolluting energy comes to the fore; and sustainable economic practices blossom.

Understanding where we have come from will help define who we are in this moment and what we might become in the future. Human consciousness sets the stage for social behavior. Deeper consciousness catalyzes cultural advances, like better parenting, that produce more intimate individuals, a more functional society, and a healthier planet. Realizing that change has always been an ongoing planetary process might make individuals and entire societies more accepting of change, especially when such realizations bring meaning to one's life. Humans aspire to meaningfulness.

Our Generation's Challenges

Our willingness to continue pumping carbon into the atmosphere, ignoring the impending loss of many more species, contaminating the world's water—this is a crisis created from lack of meaning in our everyday lives. We are not stupid. Those who are making decisions are aware that this behavior's cumulative effect is damaging the world, but personal gain is more important to them than a healthy ecology. Perhaps they believe that wealth will buffer the ever-increasing toxic environments or that their personal lives will not be affected because the damage occurs elsewhere.

Success at gathering wealth often requires intelligence; ignoring the big picture is different—it is ignorant. We have created a culture in which intelligent ignorance is rewarded; thus, a meaningless scramble for more assets has replaced our sacred-Earth connection. Social values will only change when we integrate our currently available ecological wisdom.

Large-scale Newtonian physics explains a great deal of physical reality, but on a small scale, in particle physics, the theories do not work. Newtonian science is only accurate for a limited physical reality. When applied to small particles, it is not valid. In the social sciences, particular behaviors may "work" and not damage nature when applied on a small scale, but when carried to an extreme, without interventions and adjustments, those same actions will create failure and loss. For example, a society that consumes more of the Earth than it restores is consuming its children's future. On a small scale, increasing production can benefit the species. On a large scale, it turns into overproduction and becomes destructive.

Consider this counterproductive Middle Ages medical practice: Before microscopes, infectious bacteria were unknown. Consequently, surgeons lost patients to bacterial infections and could not determine what had happened. They created "scientific" theories to explain the problem, which resulted in confused actions like "bloodletting" to address the illness—often making the patient worse. The bacteria existed, but they were as yet undiscovered. Although they are the foundation of our own cells, their existence remained "in the dark."

As with bloodletting, we can't "think" our way into Natural Harmony. The thoughts we have, for the most part, come from what we already know, from accessible consciousness. To tap into the unknown, into material that is still in the "dark realm," *is* the process of expanding human consciousness. This more often occurs from intuition, perhaps in a dream state, than from effortful thinking. Of course, thinking prepares the ground for intuition to grow.

Accessibility to all current information within a particular field is the best way to uncover or retrieve the next bits of information (one could say bits of awareness) that will advance that field. These new bits come from the heart as much as from the head. They come through the whole body, the cellular neurological receptors in the brain, yes, and also those receptors in the skin and the liver and the bowels. It is one's entire energetic cellular system that taps into Natural Harmony. Relying only on the rational thought processes, we make mistakes. In the process of finding the accurate cause of bacterial infection, we created more pain and suffering through our "thoughtful" errors.

The bloodletting example stands as a metaphor for a great deal of human history: medical, scientific, and social. Finding an immutable scientific solution is finding Natural Harmony. The Earth orbits the Sun. It was in 1543 that Copernicus correctly showed this now-obvious scientific fact and helped to usher in the Scientific Revolution. Greek philosophers might have known this a few thousand years earlier, but the wisdom was not integrated. It was an unproven theory.

How many tens of thousands of years before that did we modern-brained humans create incorrect information, trying to explain the Earth, the Sun, the planets, and other celestial phenomena? The Catholic Church persecuted Copernicus for his scientific beliefs. How many thousands of people were executed because they had a different view, right or wrong, to explain the embrace between Earth and Sun? Consider all the inaccurate but thoughtful ideas and ideals that caused war and mayhem for many thousands of years.

The scientific epoch, lasting about five hundred years, eventually created a world culture based on "mental consciousness," that is, "thinking about" began to overwhelm "participating in." Our daily activities became mental exercises that pulled us further out of nature's interactive life matrix. Asphalt, buildings, and cars replaced meadows and animals as our primary relationships. Cities produced smog-filled air; the stars were no longer part of our nightly life; and being alone at night became unfamiliar and, therefore, scary.

Farmlands became corporately owned, forcing families off the land and into the artificial cities. We no longer had to learn about a deer's habits or salmon runs in order to feed our children; repairing the automobile became the priority. We became afraid to drink water from a stream. The best spiritual connection we could muster was to "think about" God in church while the preacher told us how things really are. A life full of "thinking about" is an artificial life bereft of the natural world. No wonder we have fallen out of sync with Natural Harmony; we have lost our connection to nature itself.

Individuals have freedom of thought and action, or free will, an essential quality in finding Natural Harmony. Reflective consciousness allows us to make choices and, therefore, to make mistakes. It is this process of trial and error that leads to wisdom, to accurate scientific discovery and to correct ethical decision making. It often takes thousands of years and many experimental forms to find our way to a scientific or social "truth"; for example, we moderns get "fooled" when we look at our most recent three-thousand-year history. Lessons from this recent time frame are often all that's taught, even at our best schools, though our *Homo sapiens* story extends back about two hundred thousand years. Even this three-thousand-year history is taught using limited information—essentially, outmoded beliefs and ideas.

We seven billion-plus humans are focused primarily toward putting food on the table for our little ones. When someone does not have the time or opportunity to focus on planetary and philosophical issues, he or she is easily confused and misled. For the most part, Jesus's messages were simple and clear in the gospels: be kind, be gentle, be humble, and thereby find heaven on Earth. Soon the "church" co-opted these "social truths" for its own aggrandizement, wealth, and power, which they named Christianity. It took two thousand years to finally free Western culture from this tenacious grasp. However, "Christ-consciousness" survives because what Jesus said fits within Natural Harmony's philosophical framework. Conversely, Christian fundamentalism, like Muslim fundamentalism, is the grim reaper of mayhem and death.

Our Western culture was fooled for centuries into thinking that this church-sponsored distrust of others was "Truth." Our "economy" has fooled us in a similar way. Our simple, ingrained desire to care for our children, providing more food and safer housing, has been co-opted by the "stuff" producers, and we are easily tricked by corporations, their gadgets, and their "stuff." While corporate behavior runs amok, we are confronted with human overpopulation, climate chaos, biodiversity loss, species extinctions, decimated habitats, toxic waste, and unsustainable economic practices.

Natural Harmony

Natural Harmony is a mysterious energetic field of biological complexity that supports mutually beneficial reciprocity, the core essence forming life's all-encompassing, interrelational web. Acting in accordance with our most profound understanding of Natural Harmony is a moral imperative.

Life-forms "grow up" while intertwining during many millions of years, percolating together in Natural Harmony's container. These interactive associations provide synthesis among all things. Every Earth-being inhabits its rightful place while integrating with all other life in an exquisite array. Of course, these associations were developed over many eons long before humans entered the scene, which occurred only relatively recently. No species has survived forever. Natural Harmony will remain after the final curtain is drawn on human existence.

To live in Natural Harmony is to support others—not just our family and friends, not just human beings—all living things. It is to make decisions and take action based on what is best for all life and for the planet's life-supporting systems: the air, the water, the mountains, and the forests. Although we don't yet recognize it, we are supported by an Earth community and cannot exist in a healthy way without this mutual support. In the past seventy years, we have been consuming this sacred trust to increase human density and to accumulate possessions. The community is now suffering our excesses and falling into deterioration, yet we are mostly blind to our behavior.

Natural Harmony creates life's beauty, art, and music. This story is about human consciousness learning to integrate more fully with Natural Harmony. Planet Earth has a propensity to advance biological consciousness. The large-brained mammals are all examples. In the last few decades, human consciousness has reached a new level of awareness; however, our ingenuity has outpaced our conscious evolution. Our worldview, our attitude, and our behavior are causing planetwide deterioration. The way we see the world, our outlook, is recreating the physical world that we live in and depend on.

The destruction we are causing is forcing us to take the next step in consciousness. There are now several different worldviews competing for each human soul. This situation is a core issue in our creation story. Natural Harmony is the ethical guide for a constructive change in direction—the "Great Turning," as David Korton calls it. A change in direction is essential; only a major intervention will prevent chaos within the next five decades.

There are many techniques to individually connect to Natural Harmony and thereby participate at the forefront of this human evolution. It is the most meaningful, fulfilling, and sacred life one could pursue, so why not participate? The closer one gets to Natural Harmony, the more meaning one finds in life, the more open one becomes, and therefore the bigger one's life experiences: awe, wonder, respect, and gratitude. All this creates more personal joy, improved health, and, eventually, planetary healing. We humans are not yet wise enough to adequately express in words the meaning of life, but we can *feel* what adds meaning to life. Discovering how to live in concert with Natural Harmony is one pathway to a meaningful life. Our Creation Story examines what there is to celebrate about who we are as individuals and who we are, together, as a species. In short, it is about finding one's soul while healing our culture and our planet.

Our objective is to identify the many threads that are currently being woven into the fabric of this new reality. The human psyche is deepening into a more robust interconnection with the natural world. This richer understanding creates new respect for "Spaceship Earth's" operating systems and draws us ever closer to the Creative Source and Life's sacred nature.

Nothing less than this new consciousness will change our behavior. A cultural renaissance is in process that is revealing who we contemporary humans are in relation to the Earth community. Finding this perspective, this interrelational way of seeing the entire world, will guide our actions so that our children might inherit a healthy planet. Knowing more about our human story will catalyze the transformation into this new culture.

This book demonstrates how personal and cultural transformation can solve the challenges we face as a society and a species. It is about a once-in-a-lifetime opportunity—taking the next step in the evolution of human consciousness. It shows us how to successfully navigate our current dangerous terrain, an existential crossroads, to become a sustainable society. Participating in this process, whether we succeed or fail, provides a more meaningful personal "raison d'être." Its most important feature is a more deeply felt, sacred connection to all life.

There is both an individual and a cultural trajectory occurring; like it or not, change is upon us. The way we *see* ourselves in relation to other life and to the Earth's integrity will largely define our success or failure as a species. We are just now, after almost seven million years of biological evolution, after discovering so many secrets of the Earth's inner workings, coming to a crossroads unlike any other. To a large extent, we humans are now forming Earth's physical composition—its aesthetic.

Will we gracefully transition away from our cultural blindness into deepened awareness, resulting in a healthier affinity between humans and the natural world, or will there be chaos begotten of our desire for more consumption, more "stuff"? This is our epoch's grand inquiry. The changes are upon us. They will either be accepted gracefully through proactive policies, or an insistent Mother Earth will impose them upon us through trauma and pain. The all-important unanswered question is whether or not the inevitable changes can be accomplished without trau-matic chaos.

The moral and spiritual challenge of our time is the ecological crisis. Our generation's solutions or, alternatively, failure to act will define our social legacy to our children and all those following. Although bits and pieces are apparent, the essential cultural transformation required to avoid planetwide chaos is not yet apparent to society at large. This Creation Story will reorient us toward the sacred Earth and away from the prevail-ing production-and-consumption cultural values.

This awakening has the potential to show us how "mutually beneficial reciprocity" between person and planet is the most meaningful way to live one's life. *Conscious activism* can facilitate change: it engages the world while expressing one's most profound understanding of reality. Conscious activ-ism uses skillful means to liberate another person's compassionate heart.

Natural Harmony is an ethical mandate. It is not at odds with Christianity or with other major religions. The One God of monotheistic religions can be called by many names. For our discussion here, "God" is a Great Mystery that is best left undescribed because no words can capture its essence. Whether depicted as the image of a bearded wise man in the sky, as an amorphous energy field, or as the not-to-be-described Tao, this "It" can be taken to mean the source of all manifest things. Natural Harmony is the physical configuration of these many things. So Natural Harmony points us back to the Great Mystery, and respect for Natural Harmony becomes the guideline, the pathway, to define our ethics and inform our behavior.

This God-concept is not a reversion to primitive religion, the many gods, and it does not attempt to replace or dispute the description of God in any of the world's religions. In the time of Jesus, we were unaware of the billions of galaxies beyond our solar system. Indeed, at the historic time when each major religion began, we did not understand our place in the solar system; we were ignorant of gravity, of bacteria, of subatomic particles, of dinosaurs, and of the Big Bang beginning of the Universe. What we now know about many of these things will continue to evolve, just as our religions have evolved and will continue to evolve—not to deny the original configurations but to expand the subtleties and thereby bring us closer to God, the Great Mystery.

We are learning that everything ties together. It's all one system. It presents itself as Natural Harmony, which, when understood, is able to inform us about kinship with one another, with all living things, and with the Earth. The dynamic ways the planet "works" not only keep us alive, they also give us the capability to think with depth, to grow, and to learn more about creation. This perspective does not negate earlier worldviews, but, as with continuing scientific discoveries, it adds new dimensions to what we know and helps to discard our prior, more contracted outlook.

Natural Harmony is manifest from the Creative Source and characterized by mutually beneficial reciprocity. Ineffable Consciousness, that is, Consciousness as an entity, exists throughout the Universe. Human consciousness differs in that it is but a tiny segment of this Universal Consciousness. Humans continue to discover additional scientific information that was unknown centuries, decades, or just years before the present time; likewise, we continue to uncover new moral and ethical relationships that reveal our appropriate place in the cosmic whole.

Christ-consciousness was such an "uncovering" occurring two thousand years ago. The term *uncovering* indicates that the information is not actually "new" but is new to us humans. It is what always has been when seen from the perspective of Natural Harmony. It is all a part of Natural Harmony. It always was and always will be. Through the evolution of human consciousness, we humans uncover more and more—we discover—but not because it is a new thing, or because we have invented it; rather, all discovery is revealed out of the subtle mysteries contained within Natural Harmony.

In this model, both scientific reality and moral imperative existed before humans. Each simply reveals the depth of intimacy that intertwines all manifest things. As bits of each are revealed to us, we become wiser and shuffle off false understandings; what we believed to be true is often proven false. As we integrate these bits into our personal and cultural wisdom, human consciousness evolves.

After we humans separated from other primates almost seven million years ago, we began a long journey during which our consciousness deepened.[13] Even several million years after the primate separation, human consciousness remained in an embryonic state. We were ape-like. With each new form of proto-human, consciousness advanced. But it was not

---

13   The June 2013 *Scientific American* has a short article about a seven-million-year-old skull found in Chad about 2002. Researchers nicknamed it "Toumai" and believe this ancient individual is the oldest known hominid. If so, it means that the evolutionary line that eventually became humanity diverged from the other primates at least seven million years ago. Although Toumai had a 378 cc brain size, similar to that of a chimp, its brain had begun to reorganize toward the human structure. The paleoanthropologists who studied Toumai theorized that these brain changes might have resulted from upright walking.

Consciousness itself that advanced; rather, it was an advance wherein humans "took in" more Natural Harmony. We have come a long way, and we have a long way to go—that is, if we can get past this very dangerous period, the potential collapse of the Earth's life-sustaining capacity.

Ten years ago I was living near the ocean in Malibu, California. I kept an ocean kayak under a beach house nearby. One special afternoon, while I was dragging my kayak across the sand toward the water's edge, some friends from my cliff house above the beach, pointing excitedly, called out, "There's a whale!" I'd often thought of kayaking near a California gray whale, so I quickly pushed through the surf, climbed aboard, and fiercely paddled through the last breaking wave into the open ocean. With strong strokes I slid through smooth water toward the spouting goliath, but she kept moving away; the distance between us would not close—a decision controlled by the whale, not me. Tired, breathing heavily, I stopped. Seabirds squawked and spiraled above me, then disappeared. I could barely see land.

There was undulating silence; life became still. A thought pressed forward: "Why do I feel more alive out here? Life seems to have more depth." Again silence. Minutes passed. Out in the Pacific, the land was but a small outline. I felt vulnerable and at the same time embraced by everything around me, especially the whale, which remained nearby but unreachable. A light breeze arose, the rolling swells rising, falling. The ocean was breathing as I was breathing.

From within the enjoined breathing and the lapping water, I recognized Sophia's voice: "Losing your connection with other beings and the mysterious Divine makes life pointless. To lose one's intimate associations is to lose one's 'self' in the mundane. This whale is a sacred mystery. Material things separate us from what really matters. Each being is a thread in a fabric, woven by Earth itself. Thinking otherwise is isolating. Honor your embrace with the whole; respect each element. Essential Nature will appear to you when you just set aside contrived beliefs. Senses come alive in the natural world. Sensual intelligence resides in wild places; experiencing this sensuality expands your personal world. In actuality it is impossible to be separate from this 'whole form.' There is no such separateness, but you don't yet realize this. Your everyday waking dream-state is a confusing veil. To see the world, lift the veil and come to know who you really are. The forest, the trees, the whales, and the stars will teach you. Books about a whale are not enough. All Nature's beings have connected spirits. Reciprocity is fundamental in Nature, providing meaning for life."

At that moment, Whoosh! First came her powerful water spout above the surface, followed by the giant head and massive body, just yards from my kayak, one huge eye peering directly into my face as she passed—a visitation not to be forgotten.

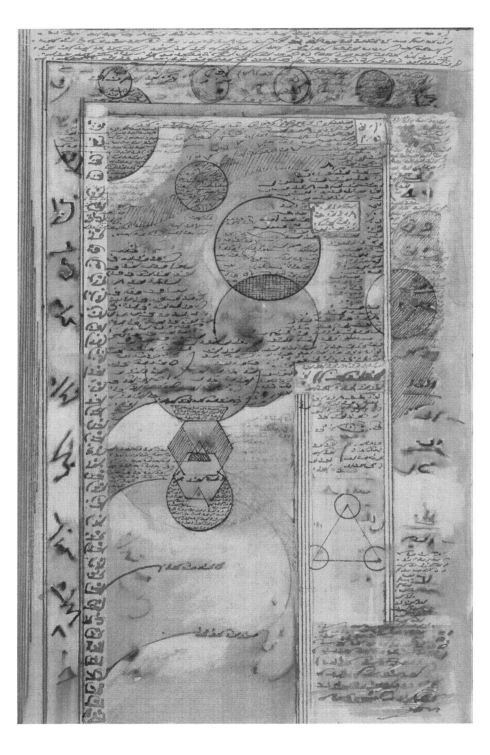

CHAPTER 9

GOD: THE GREAT MYSTERY

The Tao and its many manifestations arise from the same
source: subtle wonder within mysterious darkness.

—*Tao Te Ching*, by Lao Tzu

All creation stories (and philosophies) are working within particular boundaries—a container, if you will. The source of creation is always part of a creation story. Often this source is presented as a metaphor, providing context for an otherwise amorphous concept. The boundaries of our New Creation Story are broad ones, starting at the Big Bang and including the outer edge of our expanding Universe. God is a Great Mystery that is *not* within our Creation Story's Universe-bound realm. This Great Mystery is bigger than the Universe and grander than anything that can be conceived by any human being. God, the great indescribable Mystery, *is* part of our conversation but *not* subject to our comprehension.

The concept of God means different things to different people and varies greatly from culture to culture. The word *God* is often charged with emotions: among them are awe, fear, love, compassion, wonder, tremendousness, and even guilt. We access God through our emotions, not our minds; speaking about God is a tricky endeavor.

What does the word *God* mean in our culture? Here is a common definition: "A being conceived as the perfect, omnipotent, omniscient originator and ruler of the universe, the principal object of faith and worship in monotheistic religions; A being of supernatural powers or attributes, believed in and worshiped by a people, especially a male deity thought to control some part of nature or reality."[14] This is not the definition we shall apply in our New Creation Story; in fact, there shall be no definition whatsoever.

Various names are used throughout the world for God, the primordial being that is the Creative Source. In Hinduism, *Adi Purush* means "Timeless Being" or "Primordial Lord" or "First Person"; *Bhagwaan* specifically means God; and *Vishnu* is given a thousand names to describe his innumerable good qualities. Islam has ninety-nine names for God, representing his various positive attributes; *Allah* is the most frequently used. Zoroastrianism uses *Ahura Mazda* to name a supreme being that is "Lord of Light and Wisdom." Mormons use the name *Elohim* for God, and Jehovah's Witnesses use *Jehovah*. Native

---

14   American Heritage Dictionary of the English Language, 4th Ed., Boston: Houghton Mifflin Company, 2000.

Americans often use the term *Great Spirit* to represent the Creative Source.

The Hebrew Bible considers God's name to be sacred; so much so that any reference to God must be spoken with great care. The four Hebrew letters that are used for the word *God* would be translated YHVH in English. Some say this would be pronounced Yahweh. To me, the sacredness and careful use of God's name validates the Great Mystery of God's essence. It is improper to use the word in less-than-reverent ways because the Creative Source concept is beyond words, and any "everyday" use would debase its essence.

The *Tao Te Ching* (道德經) is said to be authored by Lao Tzu, "Old Master," who was an official at the Zhou Dynasty Court in sixth-century BCE China. *Tao* means "the Way", *Te* means "virtue combined with power", and *Ching* means "classic" or perhaps "fundamental." It is a Chinese creation myth, an ancient guide to life; it is the classic path for living, combining power and virtue. The first four lines are translated by Arthur Waley to say:

> *The Way that can be told of is not an unvarying way;*
> *The names that can be named are not unvarying names.*
> *It was from the Nameless that Heaven and Earth sprang;*
> *The named is but the mother that rears the ten thousand*
> *creatures, each after its kind.*

Another translation of the first few lines that I have remembered for several decades is: "The Tao (way) that can be spoken is not the true way."

This opening message says that the Creative Source behind the world is beyond language; it is too profound a topic to be grasped by the human mind. Something so deep or complex that it cannot be expressed in words is said to be ineffable. In many spiritual traditions, the God concept is ineffable. The third line of the *Tao* states that Heaven and Earth sprang from the "Nameless," a primordial essence that existed before time and space. It is nameless precisely because it is inconceivable and, thus, inaccessible to the human mind.

For this book I shall use a variety of terms to show that no particular cultural or religious group has a better grasp of the God concept than any other group. Why is this? We humans separated from the other primates almost seven million years ago. We grew into our anatomically "modern" physique and brain size about two hundred thousand years ago. The intellectual foundation for our current ways of conceiving our surroundings was laid about three thousand years ago. Our modern science is only about five hundred years old. Although ingenious in many regards, we humans are still infants, feeling our way in a vast Universe. We know a little, but not much in terms of all there is to know.

Our wisdom, our consciousness, is growing exponentially; the evolution of human consciousness could be said to be an inexorable movement toward a reunion with Knowledge itself, that is, toward an intimacy with the nameless Tao, the Great Mystery that is often called God. Several of the things that our creation story does *not* claim to know include what existed before the Big Bang; what our expanding Universe is expanding into; and what the catalyst is, the creative force, the primordial essence that underlies the manifest Universe.

As discussed above, many individuals, groups, and religions use the term *God* in response to the last question. I prefer to use the phrase *Creative Source*. However, to emphasize that we really know nothing about this essential question, I have also used the term *Great Mystery* interchangeably with *Creative Source*. There is support for this approach in the religious and scientific traditions. Albert Einstein was a seminal scientific genius; he was also a highly ethical humanitarian and philosopher. Putting God into an awe-filled perspective, Einstein said: *The human mind is unable to conceive of the four dimensions, so how can it conceive of a God, before whom a thousand years and a thousand dimensions are as one?*[15]

The world to which we have access is not the totality—it is not all that exists. We observe and experience phenomenal existence in isolated bits, attempting to piece together their relationships. Scientific instruments allow us to subjectively "know" a great deal about the nature of reality; however, there is so much more to which we have no intellectual access, neither phenomenally nor theoretically. Therefore, our story calls this inaccessible gestalt the Great Mystery; as it is beyond our comprehension, it is also beyond our descriptive capability.

Some think of it as God's realm. I prefer "mysterious darkness." It is our place of origin. We are continually bringing small portions of this darkness into human awareness. Indeed, our consciousness is not a passive observer of our surroundings; rather, it is continuously exploring the unknown, delving into its fecundity and using our personal creativity to illuminate these dark places. This exuberant curiosity is our special gift.

---

15 *The Expanded Quotable Einstein* (Princeton University Press), page 208.

It includes the mystical-poetic as well as the dissecting-scientific. Both polarities blend to form unity and to balance "being" with "doing."

Human consciousness stages are responsible for the depth and breadth of spirituality and religion within any particular culture. Our "God-comprehension" is a function of, and dependent upon, human consciousness levels. As our consciousness deepens, God is perceived differently than he was previously. Descriptions and God-attributes change as worldviews change. God, the Creative Source, the Great Spirit, is not changing, but our *thinking* changes, so we see God in a different light.

Finding One's Own God

As discussed, "knowing" God is actually beyond thinking; yet, for most of us, God seems to exist. For discussion purposes, our story includes three aspects of "knowing" God. These are various approaches to *experiencing* God—ways to relate to this mysterious divinity. Thinking isn't enough; however, "experiencing" often does suffice to provide various pathways for God-connection. First, within oneself resides a personal experience of divine communion, which is accessible through introspection, that is, by going inside for self-exploration. When I clear my emotions by meditating or by using other insight techniques, I am able to locate a vastness that normally invites merging and connecting. This is usually a blissful state. Emotionally and sensually I feel communion with all things. This is one definition for God—not what God "is" but rather what God feels like.

The second approach to God is thoughtful but not intellectually knowable; rather, it is acceptance of the wisdom that God resides beyond knowing.

The Creative Source exists within the dark realm. It is the unknowable Tao—"subtle wonder within mysterious darkness" in Lao Tzu's description. The world's God-given form, as presented to us in Natural Harmony, emanates from this fecund darkness. Our acceptance of this mystery provides the humility needed to feel God and act in ways that respect and support creation. The world was not created for human beings; however, we are privileged to be a vehicle for expanding awareness unlike any previous life-form on Earth. If we fail to survive, it will be at least partially because we did not "get" our appropriate interconnection with the Creative Source in time to realign ourselves with Natural Harmony.

A third divine connection comes about through appreciation and gratitude, such as that inspired by focusing on Natural Harmony, the deep association and kinship among the many million manifest things. It is awe and splendor, expressed through Nature's very existence; a Universe coming into being and expanding for 13.8 billion years; life on Earth built up over 3.8 billion years. We call our self-reflective appreciation for this vast miracle "Universe" and "Life." This is "God-ness" and will humble any person who has the courage to open to *It*.

A Universal Organizing Principle does exist. Many people believe in their own version of God and have differing ideas to describe their particular creator-entity. In many such belief systems, as the creator, God is considered to be the Organizing Principle and, therefore, responsible for the Universe's existence. In our story the term *God*, as well as the many other deity names from various religious traditions mentioned above, points to an originating essence that existed prior to the Universal Organizing Principle. This Creative Presence remains the Great Mystery.

In our New Creation Story the nature of God can best be understood from the manifest universe itself, that is, from the totality of objective and subjective reality that has been revealed to human consciousness. This manifest world is the third approach to God mentioned above. *Our story's Universal Organizing Principle is the absolute nature of reality arising as pure consciousness, intelligence, function, and beauty, which appears in objective form as all manifest things, including whales, birdsongs, human children, stars, bees and primrose flowers. As discussed previously, the relationship among the totality of manifest things is called Natural Harmony.* The objective world is organized as Natural Harmony and allows us to see the Universal Organizing Principle in operation. This principle is also revealed subjectively to the extent that human consciousness, as represented by philosophy and other intelligent ideas, is in alignment with Natural Harmony.

What seemed like magic to our grandparents is often normal to us; what seems like a miracle to us will be normal to our children. *The evolution of human consciousness is the magical and the miraculous sculpted through reason and intuition into the normal.* This origin, the mysterious darkness, is always with us because we are created by it and from it. We can't rationally "know" what it is, but we are "of" our origin, and it is within us. We are carbon-based beings, and all our carbon molecules were created inside a star—our heavenly alchemist. This first-generation star subsequently exploded and reformed into our Sun, Planet Earth, and us.

Where did we come from? Is it nontemporal and nonspatial, beyond space? Is it preexistent—existing prior to any *thing* or concept? Perhaps in this arena there is no time, just unity containing the Creative Source. These questions take us all the way back to our most fundamental, spiritual, and existential concerns: What existed before the Big Bang? What is the Universe expanding into? Are we one of many parallel universes? Are there other dimensions of existence? What is life's purpose?

Perhaps expanding animal consciousness is a biological imperative. It has advanced most rapidly in the human species and seems to grow most quickly when confronted with life-and-death challenges. Climate change and environmental destruction are providing the existential challenge that has moved us into the Ecological Epoch and, in so doing, pushed us closer to the Creative Source.

I was sitting in my everyday morning meditation practice. Unable to fully quiet my mind, I found that a question arose: "Is this me-time just greedy? Shouldn't I be doing something more productive?" The question pulled me into a still, quiet space that seemed to last forever. Time passed. Floating to the surface, an answer arose: "Introspection is a resource for those awakening to a deeper self-awareness, necessary for healing wounds of estrangement and isolation in our intimate association with our own self. Personal transformation is the first step in social change. Introspection is a valuable tool. Emotional dissatisfactions prevent you from cultivating your own potential. Even the most positive intentions, when they come from a dysfunctional emotional place, will eventually lead to negative repercussions. With intention, you can uncover hidden motivations that drive you. Self-discovery opens you to gratitude, allowing you to draw closer to the sacred source." At that moment, the Zendo bell rang, ending the session.

Dual Mind-Streams

As part of our New Creation Story I find it useful to identify two "streams" of human consciousness based on human brain physiology. Neuroscience has identified, and continues to refine, physical locations in the brain that control bodily function (for example, Dr. Lewis Mehl-Madrona's book *Narrative Medicine* does so in detail). In simple terms, it can be scientifically demonstrated that the two brain hemispheres, the right and the left sides, have different functions: the left is more language and logic oriented, whereas the right is more intuitive and mystically inclined. For our change-the-culture toolbox, we shall include our physical bicameral brain and how particular locations within it affect abstract "things" such as the nonphysical "emotional body" and, therefore, our perception of the "real" world. Worldview is critical to cultural behavior.

This complementary dual-hemisphere physical brain structure combined with what psychologists have learned about abstract structures within the psyche—Carl Jung's archetypes, for example, are discussed in Book Two—leads me to theorize that there are also dual, incorporeal, planetary information-reservoirs that can be tapped into and utilized by the human mind. Pierre Teilhard de Chardin's "noosphere" elucidates this concept, as discussed in Book Two. (It's also likely that whales, elephants, and other large-brained mammals create these information reservoirs.) These "cloud source" planetwide energetic systems affect the human psyche through interactive feedback loops. This in turn enhances human consciousness and, as a result, our ability to comprehend the nature of reality. When understanding deepens, behavior changes.

In our story, the first of these two information reservoirs is the human-generated *intuosphere*. It developed earlier in the human story than the rational; its wisdom comes primarily from the senses and intuition (for most of human existence, this was likely the primary information-processing method). For the past five thousand years or so, aided first by the invention of written languages, then the alphabetic languages, patriarchal governmental structures, and scientific method, the logical mind, called *logosphere* in our story, has come to dominate the intuitive mind. Our journey through this New Creation Story will include the cyclical rise and fall of these two information-energetic fields, intuosphere and logosphere.

This journey follows human consciousness as it weaves through the eons. Although science and rational thought have recently begun to embrace Natural Harmony, rationality has in the past been a prime catalyst for planetary desecration. There is no judgment in our story; "good" and "bad" are of no help in describing Earth's processes. Although it is useful to consider which human actions promote personal and planetary health—and the contrast between healthy and unhealthy is important—there is no "evil" in this creation story; that is part of its beauty. Both the intuitive and rational human skills represent an unfolding planetary process that could not have existed in any other configuration. Tracing these dual systems will help us follow human consciousness from its inception and better understand their potent influences.

Teilhard de Chardin was a French Jesuit priest born in 1881, but he was also much more: a paleontologist, geologist, and philosopher. His work is a beautiful synthesis, explaining Earth's living, dynamic systems in combination with our planet's sacred nature. He saw Earth as a divinely inspired manifestation of Creative Source. He wrote at least fourteen books, none of which were widely accessible until after his death in 1955. The "church fathers" repressed Teilhard de Chardin's uplifting message, one that saw life and spirit in rocks as well as in trees and people; indeed, the living Earth was the foundation for his philosophical outlook. The church decided this outlook undermined Christian doctrine. Teilhard was forbidden to publish most of his works, and he complied.

Someday, after mastering the winds, the waves, the tides and gravity, we shall harness the energies of love, and then, for a second time in the history of the world, man will have discovered fire.

—Pierre Teilhard de Chardin

The Russian philosopher Vladimir Vernadsky coined the term *noosphere*; Teilhard de Chardin further elaborated the concept. All Earth's living beings, when considered in aggregate, are called the "biosphere." The *noosphere* ("noos" from the Greek *nous*, meaning mind) is a sphere surrounding the globe (as the air surrounds the globe), containing all human knowledge. From this perspective there exists a planetwide, human-created "mind," not confined inside the physical brain of each human; rather, this noosphere is an ethereal data and information sphere. It includes complex rational constructs in addition to intuitive wisdom—an aggregated whole that is *independent* of any particular individual, although each person contains snippets of the composite, some more than others.

Teilhard de Chardin's writings were decades prior to James Lovelock's Gaia Hypothesis, but they were similar to this concept, and perhaps were an important inspiration for it. At Teilhard de Chardin's death in 1955, the World Wide Web was unknown. Today the web gives us insight into his philosophy, if we think of the increase in intellectual capacity and almost instantaneous communication the web affords us, although it is confined to computer hardware and software operating systems. The noosphere is this and much more.

Using cyberspace as a jumping-off point, we can envision the noosphere as a vast information and wisdom storehouse, surrounding the globe as an independent entity; indeed, the term *cyberspace* captures the concept as closely as possible within the popular vernacular. Although more encompassing, the term *noosphere* was also a precursor for understanding what we now know as cyberspace.

Noosphere includes not only all aggregated data and information but also its interactive "complexification," which makes it more than the sum of its parts. Data arranged in innovative ways becomes wisdom. An analogy might be the scientist who has been studying a problem for years, adding more and more knowledge to his or her endeavor, when all of a sudden, while sitting empty minded on the beach, watching the waves, the fully formed solution floods into his or her mind (many scientists do report solving problems while daydreaming or sleeping). The noosphere has the capacity to "complexify" on a planetary scale, catalyzing advances. Indeed, human consciousness is shaped by the noosphere's capacity to create deepened understanding about the natural world, catalyzing human integration with nature.

In the tradition of Teilhard de Chardin's noosphere I have coined two words to represent two collective "wisdom" fields: the intuition field (*intuosphere*) and the logical field (*logosphere*), mentioned previously. My use of italics indicates that the words, as used in this context, are meant to have an archetypal meaning, that is, these systems represent planetary "wisdom" focused in two different ways. They are fields not unlike "cyberspace" and, under the right circumstances, are accessible to any particular individual and available to all. *Intuosphere* represents composite intuitive wisdom; *logosphere* stands for all logical-rational information.

In terms of human consciousness, *intuosphere* developed first, that is, its "field" expressed itself more fully and sooner in human history than the *logosphere* field. To discuss both fields in a similar fashion to Teilhard de Chardin's noosphere, we can use both words in concert, *intuosphere* and *logosphere*, and then shorten the combination into the term *intuo-logo field*. Like noosphere, these combined fields represent aggregated human wisdom; however, any given individual is knowledgeable only about small segments.

The *intuo-logo field* is not normally balanced between its two components. In early human epochs, *intuosphere* had more influence; currently, *logosphere* dominates. Our creation story is dramatically affected by the ebb and flow created by powerful influences from these two energetic fields. When examining human cultural development, one quality is often prominent for an epoch, subsuming, overwhelming, or dominating the other.

In Book Two we shall discuss theories from anthropology and philosophy that provide tools to better understand consciousness and human behavior. *Logosphere* and *intuosphere* play an important role in this story line. Fortunately, cultural progression and changing human behavior are more cyclical and random than they are linear. If we were on an exclusively linear path, there would be less possibility of avoiding our species-wide decline: progressing from villages to fortified cities; from gunpowder to nuclear bombs; from chemical pollution to climate chaos; from local, gender-balanced societies to planet-dominating, warmongering patriarchal behemoths; from sustainable indigenous lifestyles to out-of-control, unsustainable economies.

Alternatively, in addition to the male-dominated culture of the present, there is also another, albeit currently submerged, "energetic system." This *"intuosphere field"* is the one that predominated for most of human existence. It is the primary container for the wisdom and emotions that bring us together: Eros, attraction, connection, and intimacy.

Dancing with the Divine Feminine and the Enlightened Masculine

This Creation Story describes the human condition. What on Earth does it mean to be human? Does human presence promote planetary evolution or its opposite—global devolution? In the Hindu tradition, Shiva is a supreme god who has observed all events from creation's beginning. He creates, preserves, destroys, conceals, and reveals all things. His image provides a powerful archetype—a cosmic dance that has come to Earth, allowing evolution by eliminating the old to make way for rebirth. Shiva reveals this new story by destroying our current dysfunctional worldview.

This is a mythic story of "doing" verses "being." Since the beginning of the scientific revolution five centuries ago, adolescent human consciousness has poked and prodded Mother Nature to extract her secrets. How does she function? Like any curious child, we just want to "know." But since about 1945, the time of my birth, our science-wielding adolescence has grown quite powerful. Its ingenious inventions have caused massive collateral damage. We're immersed in the patriarchal masculine archetype, steaming forward, clutching tools in the left hand, weapons in the right.

What have we lost? What is missing? In our exuberance, scientific ignorance, and excitement, we left behind the Divine Feminine. Men are not to blame for this. Both men and women allowed the Divine Feminine to be subjugated, bound and shackled to the Patriarchal Masculine. We are now searching for the key to unlock those shackles. While the search continues, the grim reaper is claiming one species after the other, like sand particles passing through the hourglass of the ages. Extinction is forever.

Procreation is a sacred process. When a culture sees all life (the colorful flowers, luminescent fish, dragonflies, elephants, and children) as sacred, then it makes choices based on respect, gratitude, and kindness. This is a state of consciousness. Our contemporary society is not in this mind-set. One reason for this circumstance is that in modern cultures, the masculine qualities dominate the feminine. This disequilibrium, combined with our remarkable scientific accomplishments, is causing great difficulty.

When did the dance between the Divine Feminine and the Enlightened Masculine begin? A long, long time ago; we are an unfolding product of 4.57 billion years of planetary evolution. We recently began our human journey by separating from the other primates about seven million years ago. Then, about two hundred thousand years ago, voilà—*Homo sapiens* with fully formed brains and bodies were walking the Earth.

As discussed in other chapters, the last ice age ended about thirteen thousand years ago. Approximately eleven thousand years ago, humans began cultivating the land. This period is called the Neolithic (meaning New Stone Age) because more sophisticated stone tools were developed. Writing was not invented for another six thousand years; however, we do have the remarkable abstract cave paintings from Altamira, Spain, and multiple other locations that coincide with the Neolithic period's beginning. Additional cave art, such as that found at Chauvet, France, dates back at least thirty-five thousand years; there are also more than 350 other spectacular European archeological sites from the Neolithic period, pre-dating written language and "history."

In addition, we have thousands of small sculptures, clay figurines, and other anthropological artifacts from the early Neolithic. The preponderance of this material indicates a high regard for the feminine qualities, including procreation, nurturing, and relationship. Exaggerated pregnant abdomens shown in many female figurines indicate respect for women's creativity, while emphasis on the female reproductive organs, the vulva and breasts, indicate the sacred nature of sex and reproduction. These paintings and artifacts help to differentiate "feminine principle" cultures from "masculine principle" cultures.

Our species comes in two genders. Consciousness seems to follow a parallel tract composed of two forms that we are referring to as "feminine" (more aligned with *intuosphere*) and "masculine" (akin to *logosphere*). Here we have an important distinction: men and women are different and, at the same time, they each have access to both these consciousness spectrums. Each individual, no matter what gender, has feminine and masculine aspects. Women are feminine first. Women more readily connect to feminine consciousness; however, concurrently, women also have full access to masculine consciousness. Likewise, men have access to both forms, even though masculine consciousness is more readily accessible to most men.

Sexual reproduction began as much as one billion years ago, which was well after life began 3.8 billion years before the present time. The distinction between female and male is even more recent. Since the appearance of these two genders, feminine and masculine characteristics have added complexity to the evolutionary process. Genetic recombination enhances reproductive variety because it mixes genes more effectively, thereby producing more species and additional evolutionary opportunities. Our planet's biology evolves; humans evolve; cultures evolve. Our Creation Story Continues:

Since civilizations began, various human cultures have exhibited more feminine or more masculine qualities. As cultures evolve, the emphasis changes. There is an optimal balance within any system. We might also say there is a healthy range of functioning in which fluctuations occur. When we move outside these boundaries, the system's health is compromised, and dysfunction results. Our culture has become unbalanced on the masculine side, and we are facing severe consequences. The past five thousand years have been male dominated—masculine principles have controlled most civilizations. In the past 150 years, ingenious inventions have appeared, allowing human population to expand exponentially. Feminine principles have been subjugated, resulting in confusion about how to utilize scientific discoveries in harmony with the Earth's living systems—the water, the air, the Earth, and the myriad life-forms.

The destruction we're causing is horrifying to individuals who can feel the loss and recognize how essential it is to maintain a healthy Earth. This pain has galvanized millions, who are now attempting to solve the challenges that have been created from ignorant overconsumption. It is these cutting-edge millions who are moving our species into the next stage of human consciousness. This circumstance has also set the stage for feminine principles to regain more cultural influence.

The Divine Feminine is about *being*. It emphasizes appreciation for beauty and love. This present-moment attitude encourages relationship, whether with one's own child, a darting goldfish in the pond, or an unusual cloud in the sky. Alternatively, the exuberant masculine is about *doing*, exploring things, building structures, and teasing out scientific discoveries. Our culture is unbalanced in favor of the patriarchal masculine that makes decisions based more on ideas than on intuition and compassionate feelings. This results in a lot of flailing around, doing this and that, all the while at a loss for the missing Divine Feminine that we so desperately want to experience.

In some respects, our molesting of Mother Nature is a perverse desire to be with the Divine—perverse because our new discoveries are not held in sacred trust; rather, they are used to make more "stuff," further alienating us from divine connection. This scientism is an awkward, adolescent attempt to embrace the subjugated Divine Feminine.

The Divine Feminine and Enlightened Masculine, qualities that are exemplified in today's wise men and women, are essential elements for humans' successful future on Earth. When there is balance, we achieve an alignment in which the Enlightened Masculine loves the Divine Feminine as a partner, releasing her from subjugation and restoring her to equal status. Natural Harmony is this marriage between the Divine Feminine and Enlightened Masculine. In this relationship, the masculine-oriented "doing" respects and supports the feminine-oriented "being."

The Divine Feminine is the great Goddess of early religions; the Enlightened Masculine is an evolved manifestation from the great God of more recent religions—a newly manifest God that partners with the Goddess as an equal. Both archetypes are needed for balance. One without the other diminishes the human spirit. They need each other to be whole.

Feminine and Masculine Qualities

The genders have existed for several hundred million years. Genetic recombination is an Earth-life strategy that has promoted healthy biological evolution. Mutations are biological experiments; some of these become new species. Humans, men and women, have only recently evolved. Carl

Jung, the Swiss psychologist, created a personality theory focused on feminine and masculine qualities. He used the term *animus* to represent the masculine qualities present in a woman and the term *anima* for the feminine traits in a man. As mentioned earlier, it is normally easier for women to access feminine consciousness and for men to access masculine consciousness; however, each person has both, in varied proportion. Cultures are similar; some are characterized by feminine qualities, and masculine ones dominate others.

For purposes of philosophical discussion, the "masculine and feminine qualities," although thoroughly intertwined in actuality, can be teased apart for separate consideration. It is useful to consider the masculine and feminine qualities, not as separate, competing categories, but rather as one spectrum that forms a unity and thereby completes itself.

What are feminine and masculine attributes, as expressed by men and women in our "everyday" lives? Childbearing is the ultimate human creative act. Creativity is first and foremost a feminine quality. At the same time, men are also wonderfully creative. Both men and women conceive architectural monuments and inspired artworks. Relationship skills, the art of intimacy and "emotional intelligence," are feminine qualities; and, although normally easier for a woman, many men are also accomplished in these arenas. As compassion and empathy are qualities that are founded in relating, these also fall on the feminine side of the scale, as does intuition—listening to the body's wisdom.

The feminine is nurturing and relational; the masculine is individually focused and goal-directed. The feminine functions in cycles, like the Moon's cycles; the masculine is linear, moving outward like an arrow.

Some women have more masculine qualities than many men have, and vice versa; however, it is more typical for a woman to exhibit feminine qualities. A mother requires patience and acceptance to nurture her screaming child, and, thankfully, breast-feeding provides a positive physiological sensation for mothers. Men nurture also; yet, considering all men and all women, we know there are differences across the nurturing spectrum.

The masculine is particularly good at *doing*. When provided with a vision from the creative feminine, the masculine accomplishes the finished product, such as a massive monument or a Moon landing. Logic, reason, and ideas fall in the masculine arena—the scientific revolution, prodding out the Earth's secrets, and pursuing idiosyncratic philosophies. The masculine is about thinking, accomplishing, pushing forward against all odds; it is strong, powerful, and brave in the face of adversity. Remember, it is not just men who exhibit these qualities. Successful childbirth also requires masculine resolve; today's many single working moms must be resolute in their *doing*. Some women are excellent soldiers. The ancient mythologies include goddesses as warriors and hunters.

Feminine and masculine qualities are utilized every day by both men and women. It normally takes men more effort to develop and express their feminine and vice versa for women and the masculine. Being and doing are different. Our mammal cousins illustrate differences among species: "busy as a beaver" is an analogy that gets applied to humans as well as beavers; at the other end of the spectrum, both male and female koala bears are the epitome of just *being*, hanging out in the eucalyptus tree all day, half stoned from its leaves, "no worries, mate."

Consider the feminine and the masculine archetypal forms: the Divine Feminine and the Enlightened Masculine. The "everyday" feminine in its most accomplished, wisest aspect is the "Divine Feminine"; likewise, the evolved masculine can be called the "Enlightened Masculine." These qualities are not human specific; they existed before humans and shall exist after humans depart the planet. Both are needed for Natural Harmony. Their integration is an important theme in our Creation Story. It is about an archetypal dance: the "everyday feminine and masculine" vying for expression, pushing for elbowroom, attempting to intervene in the human enterprise and control social behavior. Our evolution, on the other hand, is a movement in human consciousness. As we move from one consciousness stage to the next, we come closer to these pure forms—the Divine Feminine and Enlightened Masculine.

These are archetypal qualities that manifest as emotional and psychological "energy fields." In their pure form, they recognize the Earth and all its living things as sacred beings. Intuition is one defining feminine quality. Our new term *intuosphere* represents this energy field, while *logosphere* represents the masculine energy field. The masculine is more logical. Each term represents accumulated wisdom on its respective side of the scale: the creative feminine and the productive masculine.

This dance doesn't always look like a dance; sometimes it's more of a life-and-death competition. Who's taking the lead? The last eleven thousand years since agriculture began and civilizations developed have cycled through both aspects many times. These have been mostly prehistoric, mythological times. Our story follows *intuosphere* and *logosphere* as they cycle in prominence, back and forth, first one, then the other exerting primary influence on individuals and cultures. This wide spectrum of behavior is at the story's core: the feminine and masculine dancing together, competing and searching through human consciousness for their divine and enlightened aspects.

On Hawaii's Big Island, the volcano is constantly churning, and lava is always flowing to the sea. Over the past eighteen years, I have spent many days and nights on this most powerful land. Old lava fields often look like plantless Moonscapes. During the molten flow, cinder towers sometimes bubble up from the black field. After climbing up one of these ancient, ten-foot-high lava structures, I peered in and discovered a cave-like hole going down and down into the steam-venting lava tube, perhaps twenty feet below.

This was a place known only to locals. There was a stone ledge that others had used to store unnecessary clothing. Handwritten on a wood plank was a message: "Entering Pele's Temple. Leave your busy mind and opinions here—essentials only." I stripped naked and started down the wooden ladder. At the bottom I had to duck down to enter the small, steam-filled cave. Near its ceiling was a light shaft that shone through a hole in the stone wall; in concert with the steam, it was just enough to feed the moss and tiny ferns attached to the chamber's lava interior.

After sitting still on the mini-cave floor for some time, a spontaneous humming song welled up from my lower chakras to my chest and throat; this soft chanting filled the cave, seemingly independent of me. I listened to myself sing this tune of unknown origin. Eventually, the quiet chant found an ending. From the silence, questions welled up from somewhere inside my own vast universe, just as the mysterious song had done: "How can I bring more love into my life? Where are there more compassionate, kind, loving people? Where must I go to find more presence and love for myself?"

Silent now, I sat with bowed head, steam pouring in from the depths as sweat trickled down my bare chest, back, and arms, dripping from loosely hanging hands and fingers onto the lava floor. There came an answer, seemingly from the same origin as the steam: "It's not necessary to go anywhere. There is never anything missing. It's always right there and has always been there. You have not invited it before now, so you are not in touch with it. The journey does not require travel; it is to rediscover what has always been there, on the periphery, awaiting your attention—an innate knowledge, always present, ready for recognition. Love in its fundamental form is connection to the Divine Creative Source. It is a universal 'grand attractor,' emanating from original Creation and weaving among all things, large and small. Loving another, whether person, place, or thing, takes many forms, all expressing a divine mutual relatedness. There are subtleties to differentiate: sensuality, affection, appreciation, adoration, devotion, enchantment, infatuation, lust, passion, worship, yearning, and many more. Love is our emotional ally, helping us to sense Natural

Harmony and align with its Source, revealing its fundamental nature. Teach love. Build real camaraderie and community. Be with those who know about love and mutual appreciation for shared wisdom. In love, nothing is required from the other: not lovemaking, obligation, or explanation. Present-moment recognition and gratitude are sufficient."

I came back to normal awareness. The cave's light shaft had blinked out; darkness had fallen. As I was climbing out, the stars seemed brighter than I had ever noticed. I loved that— subtle love, deep love.

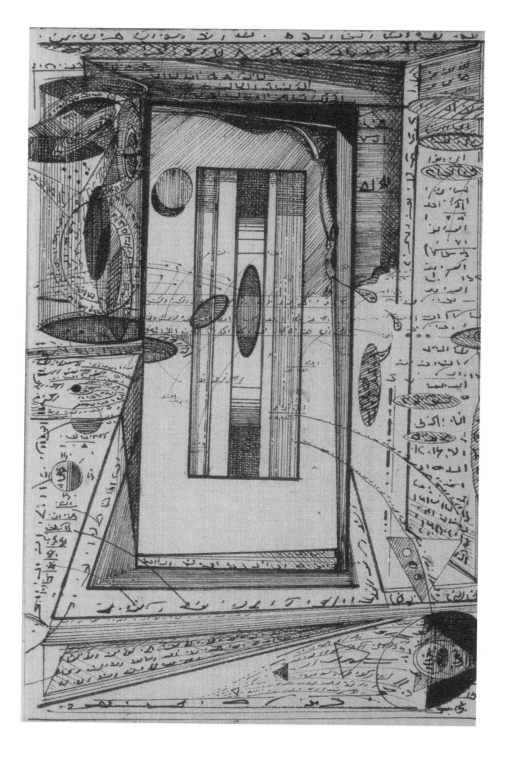

CHAPTER 10

CONCLUDING THOUGHTS: THE HUMAN EXPERIMENT

Natural Harmony Solutions

Our New Creation Story will help us to understand all that has gone wrong—some of it terribly wrong—in moving from a population of about four hundred million in the year 1400 to one billion in 1800, to seven billion in 2012, and higher now. We have set the stage for massive suffering and population decline. Our story examines what is wrong and what has recently improved; we can learn from our successes and mistakes.

The story provides a new ethical imperative: *anything that doesn't support Natural Harmony is dysfunctional and destructive.* One thing that becomes clear is that human consciousness is changing. It always has; it always will. We have recently taken the next step in the evolution of human consciousness into the Ecological Epoch. There is no right and no wrong. There is no evil and no judgment. There is no blame. The past five thousand years have featured a dance between the adolescent masculine and Divine Feminine; recently, the Enlightened Masculine has asked to participate.

> *I have repeatedly said that in my opinion the idea of a personal God is a childlike one…I prefer an attitude of humility corresponding to the weakness of our intellectual understanding of nature and of our own being.*
>
> —Albert Einstein

Is there a silver lining? In Book Three we will see how our new Ecological Epoch culture addresses its economic production-consumption challenges: how a new economy could successfully function; how we can make decisions based on the planet's health and on our respect for all other creatures; how we could value peace first; how it is possible to distribute wealth more equitably; and how we might relate to others with more compassion, no matter what continent they call home.

Communities all over the world are beginning to ban cars from some inner-city areas; what a difference it is to walk these reclaimed streets. Putting on my city-planning hat, I'm excited about all the open space that the future carless streets will provide for gardens, for parks and trees, for alternative transportation, for clean air, for massive solar panel arrays, for farmers' markets and homemade clothes, for interaction, for music on the plaza, for the celebration of life itself.

I always loved Venice, Italy, because there are no cars. Now that the rising seas are reclaiming this jewel, it is time to create hundreds of other communities without cars. Isolation reduces contacts and friends. It does not provide happiness. Social interaction adds meaning to life. The space dedicated to automobiles, including streets, alleyways, and parking, often consumes a third of the acreage within a typical city. In denser center-city areas, the percentage is higher. What an exciting opportunity, this open-space reclamation!

Sustainable economic policies are possible. We know how they can work. Local production and consumption do not need fossil fuel to transport necessities. In addition, watersheds help to define communities and could be used to establish local political boundaries so that decisions about clean water and its distribution can be made with more relevancies to the local economy. Other needed changes can be successfully instituted based on the modified free market system that already controls our economy.

In a sustainable economy, products are required to pay for their production costs, including pollution costs. For example, based on recently enacted clean water regulations, a household "cleaning products" manufacturer is no longer allowed to dump its chemical waste into the adjoining river. In the old economy, this company may have purposefully located next to the river so it *could* dump its waste into it. Remember the Cuyahoga River that caught fire near Cleveland in1969, making national news? This shocking event led to the environmentally important Clean Water Act in 1972.

It's not hard to see that eliminating this toxic waste from the river, which is a part of our "commons" belonging to the citizens, and requiring the company to bear the costs of eliminating or safely disposing of its own pollution is a move toward sustainability. Likewise, it's time for the oil, gas, auto, airline, and other companies to bear the costs of their atmospheric pollution. The air, our sacred air, has become the dumping place for all that toxic exhaust. This is a simple, straightforward, basic, and necessary "ground rule" for the new, sustainable free enterprise economy: pollution costs must be paid for by the product.

If all business enterprises were required to fully mitigate their damage, these costs would necessarily be added onto their products' selling prices, just as in the household cleaner case above. Gas might have to sell for its true cost, perhaps $20 per gallon. This is fair. This is the way our modified free market is designed to work with most products. The result would be much less driving; the auto industry would provide alternative vehicles more rapidly; there would be more local production with less "shipping"; new alternative energy industries would spring up, providing additional employment; more mass transport; and, most important, lower atmospheric CO_2—the beginning of a planetary healing process.

All this would result from the simple concept that the costs of oil, gas, coal, nuclear, and other industries should include the hidden costs associated with their pollution, atmospheric or otherwise. Of course, if this were a requirement, the companies would rapidly design alternative, less polluting products. This approach could be used for all industries. We have the technical solutions; the challenge is to find the will to implement them.

Although slow progress has been made in human rights and in environmental preservation, from a global perspective, the unsustainable production-consumption economies have created a wounded world. The scientific revolution in Europe five hundred years ago ushered in a new consciousness paradigm and different worldview, which allowed the industrial revolution to take hold about 350 years ago. New inventions provided innumerable consumer goods; more oil was required for the cars, factories and electricity plants; nuclear power and weapons spread their radioactivity, and Earth's ability to heal these industrial insults was overwhelmed. The next transformation will be based on integrative wholeness, that is, how everything affects everything else without causing harm. Sustainable economies, fewer conflicts, and a healthy Earth will be the outward manifestations.

Even our best-educated scholars know little about the human condition prior to about two thousand years ago—a time frame that is 1 percent of modern humans' existence on Earth. Put in perspective, we know almost nothing of our *Homo sapiens* story. In this case, what we don't know *will* hurt us; thus, the necessity for a closer look, which is presented in this Creation Story.

There's a documentary video that focuses on very old people, most over one hundred years old. One ancient lady, 105 years old, while talking to a studio audience, said, "People just can't see how beautiful everything is!" She had a longing in her eyes, trying to express what she felt others were missing; trying to communicate how important it is to "see" the beauty of our surroundings. There are meditations designed for this purpose. They slow us down, get us to look around—to see the light and shadow; to see the exquisite shapes all around us; to see the sky, the ground, the bird singing, almost hidden while resting on the branch; to really look at the leaf on the maple tree.

Our Story, the Human Experiment

Humans are an avant-garde species, emerging from our ancestral predecessors. Like the whales and elephants, we come directly from, and represent, all prior life in the evolutionary chain, back to the first ancestor cell—a cell that is a common relative to all complex living things. Our ancestor predecessors, the first life, appeared 3.8 billion years ago. Each iteration that added complexity has helped to build the special human-mind capability called "self-reflective consciousness". Every simple life-form that has evolved into today's complex human animal has contributed to human-held biological wisdom never before known to Earth. This awareness was not just built during the seven million years that have passed since our branching off from the other primates—it incorporates imperceptible increments over several billion years.

The human body is host to bacteria by the trillions and contains trillions of complex cells, each fulfilling a vital function that helps sustain the whole. It could be said that these cells, each with their own consciousness, trust the body to behave in healthy, functional ways that will not damage the whole or reduce its life-supporting systems. It is love's labor, this life at the cellular level. In similar ways, our many million companion species play a vital role in Earth's existence. Humans have become the dominant species on Earth. Metaphorically speaking, we have inherited a sacred responsibility from our predecessors. The trees, the plants, the animals…all life-forms have put trust in us humans. We are the advance columns, a new consciousness that has been carried forward on the shoulders of our early relatives.

Other large-brained mammals, including whales, elephants, chimpanzees, and orangutans, are similarly complex planetary experiments, equally advanced when considered in geologic time frames. A few million years is minimal to the Earth's evolutionary unfolding. This animal trust in humans is the covenant between nature and the human species. How it is managed defines our connection to the natural world. By hurting them, by destroying whales and old-growth forests, we violate them and betray their trust. When we let them down, we go down—we diminish ourselves. It's as though we are amputating one of our own arms, then a leg, truncating our body. We are collectively belittled and diminished in spirit.

I ask myself: "How would I feel if I could no longer see a flower blooming, or deer running free in the woods, or my daughter swimming in the fresh lake?" To kill when it is not absolutely necessary is to diminish one's spirit. I do not refrain from killing because of a commandment, "Thou shall not kill"; rather, I do not kill because to do so diminishes me, belittles me, leaving me smaller. I learned this as a nine-year-old, visiting a friend on his parents' farm. He had BB guns and lots of pigeons around the barn. Having never shot a BB gun, I had no real expectation of hitting a bird; I intended no harm, but my first shot resulted in one very dead pigeon. My spirit sank; I felt awful. I still remember the feeling fifty-seven years later.

Respect for Natural Harmony opens empathetic connections and a heightened sensitivity that recognizes when behavior contradicts spirit. This helps us realign with Natural Harmony. Having remorse means to "chew again" or to reexamine. It is a reassessment resulting in new cognition and realignment. For example, even violence in everyday media desensitizes us; considering children especially, exposure to these images is doing immense harm, both to the individual young person and to society at large. We become desensitized in order to block out the carnage; our broad range of feelings narrows. When we close down emotionally, we have a reduced capacity for empathy—there is less concern and desire to protect the larger community of living beings. Killing becomes easier. Spirit ebbs away, and many among us become callous, like the walking dead.

Exaggerated violence in the media is a public health problem that will delay our ability to create a healthy affinity with the Natural World. In March 2013, the *New York Times* ran a long article about media violence, stating, "The top-rated show on cable TV is rife with shootings, stabbings, machete attacks and more shootings. The top drama at the box office fills theaters with the noise of automatic weapons fire. The top-selling video game in the country gives players the choice to kill or merely wound their quarry." This destructive image-making is symptomatic of our personal discontent, our social angst, and our separation from Natural Harmony. Our films, television, and video games have become more violent over the past few decades—and are highly accessible to impressionable young minds and hearts.

Current professional research seems to be inconclusive, but my personal laboratory, that is, my own body and its sensitivities, tell me that this mayhem is desensitizing to the human spirit and one's capacity for compassion. I attempt to avoid "pop culture" media violence like I avoid contagious diseases; however, it is so pervasive that I am unable to filter out the images coming to my two young children—at school, on the streets, and even at home. While watching basketball on TV with my son, the most violent images from video games and R-rated movies are displayed as advertisements multiple times.

The mass murder of children at Sandy Hook Elementary School occurred in 2012. Events like this one are increasing in frequency compared to past decades. Although the research is not yet available to prove the case, it is likely that these episodes are correlated with the increase in violent entertainment. Given the remarkable worldwide population increase and concurrent lack of spiritual grounding, it would be expected that any modern society would create a cadre of emotionally unstable individuals. Most mass murderers are likely to be mentally unstable by definition, so the killing will probably continue until we limit access to guns, addressing the symptom, and move our sensibilities into the Ecological Epoch, addressing the disease.

Violence in media is not a true representation of life on the street or in the countryside. How many murders have you witnessed in the past year compared to those presented in the media? Violent stories have come down through the ages as myths and legends—they fascinate some people, but not others. They are attractive to certain audiences because they mirror back our fears; however, they do so with sensational hyperbole, taking remote possibilities and magnifying them until they seem like probabilities.

Fears abound, and gun sales have increased multifold; gun control has become a polarizing public debate; foreign people and religions are misunderstood and feared; our social fabric suffers from a generalized numbness; our personal world is circumscribed and contracted; and our capacity for compassion is greatly reduced. It is compassion, this connection to love and sensitivity to our real-world surroundings, that is desperately needed for the necessary transformation into the Ecological Epoch. Without this transition, my children and yours will suffer great hardship.

When we see ourselves as bigger than nature, we lose intimacy with the Earth; we neglect the unifying associations that sustain all things. When this occurs, we become smaller. We become diminished. When we use science to "force open" the sacred world, we commit a form of rape, a disrespectful penetration. When we drive species to extinction, the sacred world becomes inaccessible to us. Hence, when we behave like a bull in a china shop, we are unable to recognize the inherent sacredness that we are trampling. When we are able to see and feel Nature's beauty, creation's fullness, our own life becomes enhanced. We can "see" the life force in an ancient tree, "get" the whale's magnificence, and appreciate an endangered white rhino.

Wilderness, Fear, and Psyche

In our story Homo sapiens arrive on stage about two hundred thousand years ago. In this era we had become anatomically modern in body and in brain size. As Mother Earth ages, her offspring become more complex; we humans have been pushed to the front of this developmental experiment. We are not the best or the worst, not better than the large-brained elephants or the magnificent whales. But we are different. We have become a partner in co-creation with Earth itself. This circumstance is now central to Earth-life, as surely as the photosynthesis miracle occurring more than three billion years ago, and as surely as the first eukaryote cell, which was a necessary development for a whale to come into existence—and for the human experiment to arrive.

We humans are still an ongoing experiment with many potential outcomes. Our inventive genius has recently outpaced our wisdom; we no longer "see" our sacred nature, resulting in superficial social values. In the developed world, the culturally promoted, artificial desire for more "stuff" is so deeply ingrained that it has become insatiable. It has displaced spiritual connection and is now a hungry ghost. When we are adrift in the cosmos without connective tissue, greed and accumulation serve as distractions from deep-seated, existential fear.

Accumulating "assets" and power over other living beings is not a meaningful culmination for life's 3.8-billion-year development. The Earth has laid the groundwork for this potentially grand advance in consciousness; the human species is the vehicle that has been given the first opportunity to rationally experience a profound revelation—a deepened comprehension about biological presence on the Earth and in the Universe. This is occurring individual by individual but has not yet reached the critical mass needed for cultural change. Its voices are everywhere; its bright vision and brilliant solutions are available to counter the wanton destruction caused by our ingenious inventions and overzealous "productivity." Currently, economic consumption is tearing apart Earth's connective tissue. Using ecological consciousness, we are trying to behave differently.

About eleven thousand years ago, our ancestors began to settle in villages; plants and animals were tamed; walls arose to fence out the "wild" and the dark. Even the forest became feared—out of bounds. Light and dark were no longer complimentary forms with blended edges merging one into the other. The shadow areas between dark and light used to be a friendly habitat; however, as we "tamed" ourselves, night's stark darkness became something scary and "other." Good and evil became a black-and-white proposition, adding additional fears.

Creation stories with hells, devils, and witches were invented to stand in for amorphous death terrors. Fear of the dark is the original fear of "other," and both grew apace. Religions came to vilify "otherness," creating projections to personify vague survival fears and to justify burning their victims at the stake. When wild wolves attacked domestic cattle, they were associated with witches' spells and "werewolves"; they were purposefully exterminated and almost eliminated. In Europe, Earth-honoring "pagan" people were burned alive and otherwise executed by church edicts for approximately three hundred years, from 1450 to 1750. Millions suffered. Attempts to allay these fears have led us to our current conundrum: we fear those who are not like us. We cope by finding solace in "things," accumulation and consumption, wars, games, and television to distract us from the present moment.

Appreciation and Compassion

One achieves expanded awareness through the mind, yes, but even more through the senses: through feeling what the Earth wants from us; through combining heart-full-ness with scientific endeavor so inventions are relational as opposed to destructive; through giving the poets and artists as much influence in society as the businessmen and politicians; through making ecology the priority in economic decision making; through the meaningfulness generated in one's own life when the Earth is felt as a sensuous, sacred body to be loved. Easier said than done?

There are many methods to help. One is to focus on the beauty: appreciation for a flowing mountain stream or a two-hundred-foot-high sequoia tree—perhaps just "being" with an underwater coral reef and its brilliant, multicolored tropical fish. Allow one's primitive self to commune with one's reflective-mind-self. When we clear away our industrial society influences, the wisdom of the ages will be waiting. New scientific information combined with primitive indigenous knowledge can show us the way through this challenging epoch. A new culture will emerge: one of listening to the Earth talking, and to those people who speak eloquently on its behalf. Brian Swimme is a poetic cosmologist and brilliant author, and our story borrows an idea from one of his metaphors—bonding between Sun and Earth.

More than three billion years ago, the chlorophyll molecule was invented, not by smart human scientists with big brains but by Earth's "desire" to form a more profound bond with the Sun. Chlorophyll makes photosynthesis possible, which in turn becomes the dynamo that energizes almost all life-processes on Earth. Plugging Earth into the Sun in this manner began the photovoltaic interconnection that powers life on Earth, allowing life to endure and evolve over billions of years. Eventually, single-celled life developed into large-brained mammals. Evolving consciousness is the protagonist in this story. Concern for other beings is one quality that is highly expressed with mammals: the bonding between mother and offspring is powerful. The mother-child mammalian bonding has grown even stronger in human culture. As Homo sapiens' consciousness expanded, so did our capacity for deepened connections. We became more complex in other arenas also. Intellectual skills were added to the emotional and sensual connections—poetry appeared, integrating the entire gestalt.

I've learned that this deepening applies to fathers also; to be more specific, I have two young children, Leo and AnaSophia. Before having children at age fifty-seven, I enjoyed children; I had nieces and godchildren but never felt bonded to any particular child. The sensual depth of connection to my children is beyond anything I had experienced before Leo came along. This special connection came to the surface soon after his birth. I'm guessing from observation that the bonding is even more powerfully felt in their mother. This heart-opening love also expanded my already vital concern for animals and the forests and for keeping the planet healthy. Fatherhood created an even stronger desire to protect the Earth; yes, for my children's sake, but also for the planet's entire community of all life.

I'm suggesting that compassion, meaning "suffering with," has reached new depths with the modern human, albeit not the entire culture as yet. It is currently helping us learn about kinship and intimate connection with others. Our evolving consciousness is strengthening this hypothetical "compassion gene." We are in a "crash course" to understand all life, not just humans. It is not necessary to literally be a mother or father. Compassion combined with growing consciousness may be a powerful enough influence to pull us through our current crisis-moment, to guide us to behave in more productive and protective ways. The Earth's healthy functioning is at stake.

It is hard to be optimistic in the face of our current dilemma, but there is hope. When we learn to see through the social distractions, such as resource wars, violent media, and killer video games, among other consumer propaganda, we will be able to attend to our surroundings and their glorious beauty: glacial peaks, mountain goats balancing on sheer cliffs, and pelicans gliding along the crests of breaking ocean waves. Paying attention and feeling gratitude is one pathway to this connection. Sit still in the dark woods for a time; see how long it is before the animals trust you and allow you to "see" them. Experiences like this will change you and change the world. *The evolution of human consciousness is a movement toward greater coherence.*

The conceptual grounding of our creation story is Natural Harmony: mutually beneficial reciprocity woven into life's matrix. Natural Harmony is the epitome of coherence. Life is attracted to life because all life is bathed in Natural Harmony, not by planning and decision making but because living things developed symbiotically over vast time spans. Our story calls this energy-field-attraction by the ancient name *Eros*, as derived from the Greek creation story, Hesiod's *Theogony*. When we connect to Eros, we realize that we are vital elements of an inseparable whole; knowing this, we seek to satisfy our desires in the context of the larger Earth-body.

At times, when my creativity is stale and inspiration is hard to come by, I like to go out into the world among other cultures. There is always new stimulation awaiting me. My social "activist" group, EarthWays, has had various projects in South America over the past twenty years. Some time ago I was traveling to the Peruvian Andes where we were working with a local doctor named Pepe. He was the only doctor to serve twenty-six villages in this difficult-to-access terrain. He attempted to visit two villages each day, allowing him to return twice a month to each location. Once in a while I would accompany him. Not all the communities were accessible by four-wheel-drive jeep, so it was often necessary to hike for the last few miles. Upon recognizing the beloved Pepe, the local children would shout excited welcomes, then trail along behind, the procession growing as we progressed along the walking trail. It eventually resembled the Pied Piper's entourage.

By world economic standards, these villages were impoverished, but they had a strong family life and were in spectacular natural settings at ten thousand feet high in the Andes. There were no televisions, no cars, and no advertisements. That mountain world and those simple people with their brightly colored clothes and round, flat-rimmed hats were knitted together with love. For me, oxygen was scarce; life slowed down. I remembered more dreams.

Lying awake in the wee hours, a question presented itself: "Why does love seem so powerful here?" The answer came in my dream later that night: "Thousands of years ago, in ancient Greece there was a mythological story that described the Universe's origin. In the beginning there was only chaos. Then Eros was the first to emerge from that chaos. Eros is the underlying bonding, a loving connection inherent in all differentiated 'things' and beings. Out of chaos, given form by Eros, our planet's air, fire, water, Earth, and life force were woven together. Eros is the attraction between Earth and Sun, among all planets in the solar system, and among the galaxies—all somehow retaining equilibrium while the universe expands into the unknown. Eros is also the attraction that holds the tiniest quantum particles while they transform from matter to energy and then into newly created matter once again; it is the love you feel for your children and for the many children you have never met.

"As with the galaxies, each person's attraction to the many is maintained while she grows wiser and her own expansion unfurls; one's love embraces more and more as one's conscious-ness grows. With Eros there is a personal, erotic energy field that extends outward from oneself to encompass the many: one's immediate family; all the people, everywhere; trees in the city; the dark forests; singing birds; majestic mountains; ocean life; the wild and the wilderness—an entire multitude."

As we end Book One and transition to Book Two, our story has covered numerous long-lasting epochs from the Big Bang to the emergence of *Homo sapiens* as recently as two hundred thousand years ago. We have set the stage to examine the evolution of human consciousness in detail. This follows in Book Two, as does a look at early civilizations, mysticism, and philosophy. In our story:

The Earth was born 4.57 billion years ago; life on Earth began 3.8 billion years ago; our primate foreparents separated from our great ape relatives about 7 million years in the past; and then, very recently, the modern human appeared. These first Homo sapiens had the capacity for our greatly enhanced consciousness, but it would take the entire two hundred thou-sand years to evolve today's reflective and remarkably creative minds. Beginning from single cells, all animal species evolved from common ancestors, over billions of years, through innu-merable physical stages. In the womb a human fetus develops through similar forms: initially a single cell; later, a fishlike stage; then an early mammal form; and eventually, a minihu-man is born. Consciousness is similar. Each person develops through all earlier stages. Personal consciousness recapitulates all Homo sapiens' stages. Advancing human consciousness is not superior consciousness, so the term "higher consciousness" is misleading. All earlier Homo sapiens epochs, starting with archaic humans, provided a foundation for later stages to emerge. We are indebted to this accumulation process. Today's leading-edge consciousness is a blended consciousness utiliz-ing and incorporating all prior forms.

Subjectivity and Consciousness

Human consciousness is changing and has always been changing. The process is a slow one, so we don't "see" it happening. Focusing on the most recent three thousand years is not enough. We have discussed the "hominid epoch" beginning with our separation from other primates and extending to modern humans, two hundred thousand years before present time. In Book Two our Creation Story examines humans consciousness via changing epochs, using a classification system that starts seven million years in the deep past.

The information presented earlier about hominids and *H. sapiens* is pri-marily objective, that is, constructed from the best available facts. A more subjective approach adds texture to our consciousness-canvas. Perhaps we can achieve this with a thought experiment. Reading these pages is primarily an intellectual exercise; however, personal transformation is usually accomplished through more visceral, felt experiences. For example, falling in love is not intellectual.

Likewise, loving the forest is a visceral feeling. Let's imagine a time extending back a few million years ago; your foreparent traveled within a small troupe, in a time without access to fire. What was her world like? How did she view her surroundings? What fears drove her? What pleasures soothed her day? What foods could she eat? How did she stay warm? I'm not going to try to answer these questions, because your imagination of these conditions is as good as mine. My point is that this circumstance molded her consciousness—how she saw and felt and thought—how she perceived the world around her.

Now, let's take a step forward in time to a similar-sized band two million years later—about one hundred thousand human generations, enough time for mutations, brain development, and natural selection to produce multiple new possibilities. Perhaps these individuals have recently learned to control fire. They've yet to learn how to make fire with flint or from the friction of twirling sticks, but have learned how to save a coal from a fire started by lightning. A special member protects this burning coal in a covered vessel while the group moves from place to place to find food. They have become "fire-people" for the first time. Imagine yourself as a member of this group. The live coal is your tribe's most valued possession. An enormous bonfire is the priority and primary activity at each new encampment.

Let's stop reading for another moment. Take a deep breath and imagine how the world looks to this foreparent. Ask the same questions: What is the world like now? In what ways do her surroundings seem different? What fears drive her? What pleasures soothe her day? What foods are available to eat? How does she stay warm? In this new era many fears from eons past have been replaced by different concerns. Confidence and security have grown. Interactions with the surrounding wild animals have changed. Foods can be cooked. Warmth is more accessible, so geographic range is expanded, and new worlds are opened. More time is available for rudimentary contemplation and for expanding intuition; consequently, more discoveries are made.

A Personal Analogy

My daughter, AnaSophia, is seven years old as I write. Somewhere along the evolutionary curve, there was a hominid adult group, our direct ancestor, with a somewhat similar mental capability. Can you remember events from your own seven-year-old life—perhaps from the second-grade classroom or riding on the bus to school for the first time? Or a trip your family took. You are alert; you have good communication skills, but not akin to an older child of, say, twelve years; you engage in magical thinking (the tooth fairy is still real and anything can happen, unlimited by scientific principles), not linear rational thinking; you have limited tool-making ability, but you are good at using some tools.

Now consider all of this seven-year-old awareness inhabiting a strong, full-sized adult body. Although brain size is not by any means the only determining factor for intelligence, it may be useful to compare our recent *Homo* ancestors' brain size with that of a child. Modern human brain development grows from about 700 cc in volume in the first few years to between 1150 and 1400 cc in the midteenage years, at which time there is a "synaptic pruning" that slightly reduces brain volume.

H. erectus, from whom we may be descended, is a recent relative. *H. erectus* is thought to have had a brain size of about 1000 cc in volume. *H. erectus* may have descended from *H. habilis*, whose lineage goes back 1.9 million years. *H. habilis* had a brain size of about 800 cc. Staying with our seven-year-old-child example, we can hypothesize about the mental acuity and conscious awareness of *H. erectus*, whose members walked the planet for perhaps a half million years until about 1.3 million years ago. I observe my seven and nine-year-olds' mental activity carefully; their brain size is passing through the range of their ancient relatives, *H. erectus*. This brain-size analogy is not scientific but has some validity; admittedly, it omits other variables, such as neural networking that takes more than seven or nine years to develop.

Seven-year-olds are impulsive; have pretty good language skills; have some musical ability; are physically very competent; relate well, but primarily in egocentric ways; have pretty good, if limited, rational problem-solving abilities; are loving but impetuous and can anger easily; and can use tools they find or are given. In general, they are delightful little people. Imagining these rational and emotional qualities in an adult body might help us approximate the awareness level of *H. erectus*—good with stone tools and hunting, capable of controlling the use of fire and making clothes from animal skins, but nowhere close to figuring out how to smelt copper and tin into bronze.

I encourage you to close your eyes and carry out another thought experiment, imagining small groups of seven-year-olds in adult bodies roaming together to hunt and gather food. Try to go back to your own seven-year-old memories to find the level of awareness available to these groups. In your imagination, become a member of this nomadic band. I suggest it as a way to tune into a different consciousness than your own—again to show that consciousness has always been changing and continues to change. It is changing now.

In our creation story, consciousness transformation is an ongoing process; its exact character is less important to the story than the reality that *change is continually occurring.* The changes are not entirely linear, but the overall trend adds depth and complexity over time. Once a new stage has been achieved, it does not "go away"; however, it may be lost from a particular culture or region; people may forget the wisdom their parents once knew. Wisdom is lost; wisdom is rediscovered.

Human consciousness taps into, and is amplified by, a greater, more-than-human consciousness, which imbues all matter to some degree: rocks, plants, snakes, and humans. This grand awareness finds greater opportunity to be expressed as organisms evolve and become more complex. The large-brained mammals are currently at the apex of this complexity. Self-reflective consciousness is, so far, unique to human beings. As we shall see as our story continues, there is a "cosmological imperative" that drives both biological evolution and consciousness evolution. Human spiritual development is codependent with deepening consciousness.

Surely consciousness "complexification" is also happening on other planets and moons throughout the Universe; after all, there are many million celestial bodies with conditions suitable for life, even carbon-based life, as we know it. Human consciousness is growing toward the ever-present, omniscient, disembodied, universal "knowing." This larger consciousness could be called *Universal Consciousness* of which we humans have access to some minor, but growing, fraction.

> *The religion of the future will be a cosmic religion. It should transcend personal God and avoid dogma and theology. Covering both the natural and the spiritual, it should be based on a religious sense arising from the experience of all things natural and spiritual as a meaningful unity.*

—Albert Einstein

Universal Consciousness

Is "consciousness" only an internal quality of animal (and possibly plant) life, or might it be considered more substantial, in and of itself? Did consciousness exist before the Earth's chemicals created the first life? Has evolution been driven by a thing called "consciousness" that has its own impetus, a "desire" if you will, to express itself in larger and grander form? If so, the more far reaching term, Universal Consciousness, comes into play.

In our New Creation Story, Universal Consciousness exists throughout the cosmos; perhaps Universal Consciousness is the very thing that paves the way for spirituality to be received and to deepen within the human emotions and psyche; indeed, this viewpoint is similar in some respects to Hindu tenets and has also been explored by various Western philosophers, whom we shall meet in Book Two. Universal Consciousness has had a fundamental influence on human origins and on evolving human nature.

Universal Consciousness exists within and beyond our Earth-home; it is omnipresent and spans the cosmos. It cannot be fully comprehended. It is as mysterious as the Tao or the Creative Source. Perhaps it is a "universal mind," of which a small but growing portion has been revealed to us humans. We are a curious species driven by a biological imperative to go deeper, learn more, and integrate with our surroundings; we continue to coax out ever more consciousness from the Universe's dark, fecund, not-yet-known realms. What we currently know, this tiny fraction, is what we call human consciousness.

Life expresses Universal Consciousness. Human spirituality comes about from the deepened comprehension made possible by the evolution of human consciousness—a continual process of absorbing more and more Universal Consciousness over time. It is a step-by-step incremental unfolding. Book Two, *Consciousness*, focuses on evolving human consciousness as the driving force behind our species' continuing development.

> *The intellect has little to do on the road to discovery.*
> *There comes a leap in consciousness, call it intuition or*
> *what you will, the solution comes to you and you don't*
> *know how or why.*

—Albert Einstein

APPENDIXES

Appendix 1

The oldest evidence of a multicellular fossil, the Francevillian Group Fossil, dates from 2.1 billion years ago, which is about 2.5 billion years after the Earth came into existence—it took more than half the Earth's existence to produce this remarkable new life form.[16] Another billion years passed as multicellular life became differentiated. A red alga dating to 1.2 billion years ago has the oldest known specialized cells and is able to reproduce sexually.

Appendix 2

How does photosynthesis work? There are entire books written on this not-yet-fully understood energy-making process, so critical to all life. In its

---

16 See Abderrazak El Albani, Stefan Bengtson, Donald E. Canfield, Andrey Bekker, Reberto Macchiarelli, "Large colonial organisms with coordinated growth in oxygenated environments 2.1 Gyr ago," *Nature* 466 (7302) (July 2010): 100–104.

simple form it can be represented by the following equation for photosynthesis in plants:

$$6\,CO_2 \;+\; 6\,H_2O \;\rightarrow\; light \;\rightarrow\; C_6H_{12}O_6 \;+\; 6\,O_2$$

Carbon dioxide   +   water in the presence of light yields

sugar   +   oxygen

Upon obtaining carbon dioxide through its leaves from the air, using its chloroplasts the plant is able to convert photons obtained from sunlight into energy: some of this energy breaks apart water molecules to obtain electrons needed to convert the carbon dioxide into organic compounds. CO_2 and water are broken down and their atoms recombined into sugar while releasing oxygen back into the air. The sugar is stored energy to be used for metabolic processes. These include bodybuilding utilizing carbon compounds obtained from the CO_2.

Appendix 3

Several major developments events changed the course of life on Earth: Photosynthetic cyanobacteria proliferated to the extent that they were able to "oxygenate" the atmosphere. Oxygen at concentrations of 20 to 25 percent was toxic to most prior life forms that had evolved without oxygen. Today's oxygen percentage is 21 percent. In the past (or the future) if it goes above 25 percent, even damp vegetation would burst into fire when struck by lightning, so 25 percent is considered an upper limit.

Bacteria, perhaps as a result of their rigid cell walls, were unable to grow into large cells, most likely because of energy constraints—without membrane walls allowing for more complex structures, they could not provide enough energy to support increased size. New life prospered in forms that could use oxygen. Much earlier, Archaea cells had formed eukaryote cells with cell membranes instead of rigid walls. By utilizing the newly available atmospheric oxygen in their metabolism, eukaryotes could become large cells, many times bigger than bacteria.

Appendix 4: Extinction Events

A number of major "extinction events" have occurred in the past 542 million years—the point when complex macroscopic life began to proliferate. These occurrences refer to large life-forms only, because it is so hard to measure effects on microscopic life due to paucity of fossil records. An extinction event is a sudden occurrence that results in a much larger species disappearance than would be normal over the course of time (normal rates are called "background extinction rates"). There have been at least five, and perhaps twenty, extinction events since the beginning of the Cambrian period, depending on the definition used. Considering a 50 percent loss of species for our definition, there have been five events starting with the Ordovician-Silurian extinction 450 million years ago. As discussed in other chapters, we humans are well on our way to creating the sixth extinction event.

About 450 million years ago the Ordovician-Silurian extinction resulted in 57 percent of all genera disappearing. The Late Devonian extinction, in which about 70 percent of all species were lost, occurred about 370 million years ago. As discussed in Chapter 7, the Permian-Triassic extinction from 251 million years ago was called the "Great Dying" and opened the way for a new life-community. After dinosaurs' rise to prominence, the Triassic-Jurassic event from 205 million years ago killed off most of their competition, providing room for their further expansion. Lastly (until now), the Cretaceous-Tertiary extinction that ended dinosaurs' reign occurred about 65 million years ago. Space was now opened for mammals to proliferate. Birds, which are surviving forms of dinosaurs, also greatly expanded their species in this new world.

When it comes to differentiating individual species, life forces appear to move in the direction of more sophistication and greater diversity. When diversity is low, for example after a major extinction event, there is pressure toward adding more species; when life is abundant, species extinctions eventually become more numerous. It is theorized that there are long periods when the entire community of life on Earth is under duress—when the climate is changing, for example. From the fossil records, low-grade ongoing stress does not appear to be enough for a mass extinction; however, when combined with a sudden shock to the system, an asteroid hit for example, there can be a sudden collapse in the number of life-forms. Without the long-term stress, a sudden shock is not necessarily catastrophic. It is fair to say that our current industrial society on Earth has created stressful conditions for the planet's living systems. Considering additional "shocks" to the already stressed systems: Japan's major earthquake in early 2011 caused a tsunami and nuclear reactor meltdown at Fukushima. These events were thought to have had an extremely low probability of occurrence. What is the statistical likelihood of a major volcano adding a "volcanic winter" to the current climate stress?

Long-term stress can occur in a variety of ways: "flood basalt" events occur when massive amounts of lava flood out from below the Earth's crust, covering huge areas thousands of square miles in size. Sulfur dioxide and other particulate material are released into the atmosphere to such an extent that food chains are disrupted; resultant "acid rain" can poison environments and CO_2 buildup can change the climate rapidly. Huge volcanoes can have a similar effect by reducing plants' ability to photosynthesize and, thereby, reducing or eliminating herbivores' food sources. As herbivores decline, so do carnivores. This was the most likely cause of mass extinctions at the end of the Cretaceous period about 65 million years ago, the Permian about 251 million years ago, and the Triassic about 205 million years ago.

Sea levels rise and fall over geological time frames, sometimes as much as hundreds of feet. Raising water is often caused by climate change, with higher concentrations of CO_2 causing warming, thereby expanding ocean-water volume in addition to melting glacial ice. Falling water levels are caused by climate cooling and increased glaciations; falls may also be caused by tectonic plate movement causing sinking in the midocean ridges. Shallower water depths at the continental shelves harbor the greatest number of open-water species. Wetlands next to the shore serve as nurseries for a large percentage of the marine ecosystem. These environments change drastically with major sea-level changes, especially with the lowering of sea level, which strands the wetlands and much of the continental shelf area. It is also possible that sea-level rise and fall accentuates whatever climate change is already occurring, creating a more dramatic impact. All the five major extinction events referred to in the paragraphs above were associated with sea-level falls.

Like volcanoes and flood basalt events, asteroid impacts can create such force that massive amounts of particulate matter are vaporized and thrown into the atmosphere, blocking out the Sun's rays for years at a time before settling back to Earth. This disrupts almost all food chains, and many species perish. In addition, sulfur exploded into the air mingles with water vapor and returns as acid, poisoning some ecosystems. Tsunami waves and massive forest fires may also occur from these events. Only one impact event has been associated with a major extinction, ending the Cretaceous period about 65 million years ago and causing the dinosaurs' extinction. It should be noted that ongoing research indicates a significant time lapse between the asteroid strike in the Yucatan Peninsula and the eventual extinction spasm that claimed the dinosaurs; therefore, the full mechanism of their disappearance has not been entirely resolved.[17]

In addition to sudden events like volcanoes and asteroids, long-term climate change dramatically affects the Earth's dynamic systems. The amount of freshwater circulation in the rainfall cycle is increased when global warming occurs, as more water is evaporated into the air; conversely, rainfall is decreased with a cooling climate as a result of lower evaporation and increased "permanent" ice. Over thousands of years these environmental changes cause extinctions.

Understanding of extinction spasms has become available only recently. Knowledge of prior extinction events was unavailable to ancient

---

17 See sources: W. Bottke, D. Vokrouhlický, D. Nesvorný, "An asteroid breakup 160 Myr ago as the probable source of the K/T impactor," *Nature* 449 (2007) 48–53; D. Majaess, D. Higgins, L. Molnar, M. Haegert, D. Lane, D. Turner, I. Nielsen, "New Constraints on the Asteroid 298 Baptistina, the Alleged Family Member of the K/T Impactor," JRASC (2008).

philosophers. It has not been incorporated into prior creation stories, at least not explicitly—one might say that the Hindu Lord Shiva, embodying creation and destruction, is an implicit representation of "death" and "rebirth" that occurs from an extinction spasm. The Old Testament story about the flood and saving the animals on Noah's Arc is more about a "dying off" and recovery of humans than about extinction. Our current story needs explicit extinction information because it attempts to define our human origins as specifically as possible in order to discern who we really are.

We are one animal species. We are catalyzing the largest extinction in 65 million years. Best estimate is that 25,000 species are going extinct every year. The normal "background" extinction rate would be about one per year, were it not for human activity. And as a collective, humans are not really aware of it. Except for a very small percentage of people, the information has not sunk into our consciousness.

Appendix 5

Our family tree and the relatives who did not make it: Sahelanthroposus tugenensis (6.5 to 7 million ybp); Australopithecus anamensis (3.9 to 4.3 million ybp); A. afarensis (3.2 to 3.8 ybp) and contemporary Kenyanthropus platyops; K. rudolfensis and A. africanus and P. aethiopicus all overlap somewhat (about 2.0 to 3.0 million ybp); H. ergaster, and Homo habilis, and P. robustus and P. boisei also overlap (about 1.5 to 2.5 million ybp); H. cepranensis, and H. erectus, and H. mauritanicus overlap (about one million ybp); H. heidelbergenis about 500,000 years ago is thought to be the direct ancestor of H. neanderathalensis (alive until 30,000 ybp) and of us Homo sapiens; H. floresiensis is also a recently living side-branch, not in our direct line.

Appendix 6

The bones' ages were determined from volcanic deposits in the same strata that had been previously dated with precision to 3.4 million years old. The article reports that the bones were analyzed by "microscope and elemental analysis using secondary electron imaging and energy dispersive x-ray spectrometry" to show the cut marks' origin, clearly indicating cutting and scraping for flesh removal and pounding for marrow extraction. The *Nature* article informs us that scrape marks on bones from two animals, one pig sized and one cow sized, show clear evidence that stone tools were in use. The bones' ages can be deduced from the surrounding geological features in which they were imbedded. Prior to this discovery there was evidence of cut-marked bones in Ethiopia dated to 2.5 million years ago, and large cashes of actual tools from 2.5 or 2.6 million years ago confirms the bone evidence.

Appendix 7

Acheulean tools took time to spread throughout various communities of hominid species, for example, not reaching Europe until five hundred thousand years ago, perhaps a half million years after the tools first appeared. Although appearing in India, these tools may have never gotten to Asia where *H. erectus* continued to use the original Oldowan tools until the species became extinct about two hundred thousand years ago.

Mousterian tools were developed about two hundred thousand years ago, primarily in association with *H. neanderthalensis* in Europe, and later in the Near East and Africa where Acheulean tools were in use. They were also made by *H. sapiens*, possibly after adoption from the Neanderthals. The very close proximity in time of the anatomically modern human two hundred thousand years ago and the development of more sophisticated tools should be noticed, even if contemporary Neanderthals were the primary inventors. What was new? The stone to be used for a tool, the core, was itself initially prepared so that multiple wedge-shaped sharp tools could be "knocked off" this core; then these rough, sharp-edged, large "flakes" were refined into different uses in standardized ways—the first Model T of the tool world. With larger cutting surfaces, these tools lasted longer and could be sharpened by reshaping after long periods of use. Sharp points were made, some with a flared bottom stub for attaching to spears. Stone points were combined with wood lances and spears; horns and bones were incorporated into new tool and weapon forms. Serrated cutters were made as well as better scrapers, all of which made the manufacture of shoes, clothes, and hide shelters more efficient and effective, eventually contributing to modern human's creature comforts and more complex social organization.

The final advance in Paleolithic toolmaking occurs in the Upper Paleolithic, although these tools, called Upper Paleolithic tools, first appear as long ago as ninety thousand years in Africa. They became widespread about forty thousand years ago. Sewing needles and fishhooks appear. In different regions and different habitats, similar, recognizable tools have the same characteristics, including specialization in materials, function, and form. Many of these specialized tools are utilized for obtaining additional food sources.

More refinement occurs in the Aurignacian period about forty thousand to twenty-eight thousand years ago among Neanderthals and *Homo sapiens*. Continuing development occurs after the Neanderthal extinction, called the Gravettian period, where blades have backing and sharpened bone points are utilized. New technology is used to produce Solutrean tools for about three thousand years, followed by delicate refinements in the Magdalenian period, ending about twelve thousand years ago, near the beginning of the Neolithic.

BIBLIOGRAPHY

Abram, David. *The Spell of the Sensuous: Perception and Language in a More-than-Human World*. New York: Pantheon Books, 1996.

Armstrong, Karen. *A Short History of Myth*. Edinburgh, New York: Canongate, 2005.

Begley, Sharon. *The Plastic Mind*. London: Constable, 2009.

Berger, Lee R. *In the Footsteps of Eve: The Mystery of Human Origins*. Washington, DC: National Geographic Society, 2000.

Berman, Morris. *Coming to Our Senses: Body and Spirit in the Hidden History of the West*. New York: Simon and Schuster, 1989.

Berry, Thomas. *The Dream of the Earth*. San Francisco: Sierra Club Books, 1988.

————. *The Great Work: Our Way into the Future*. New York: Bell Tower, 1999.

Brower, David Ross. *Let the Mountains Talk, Let the Rivers Run: A Call to Those Who Would Save the Earth*. San Francisco: HarperCollins West, 1995.

Brown, Lester R. *Eco-economy: Building an Economy for the Earth*. New York: W.W. Norton, 2001.

———. *Plan B 3.0: Mobilizing to Save Civilization.* New York: W.W. Norton, 2008.

———. *Plan B 4.0: Mobilizing to Save Civilization.* New York: W.W. Norton, 2009.

———. *World on the Edge: How to Prevent Environmental and Economic Collapse.* New York: W.W. Norton, 2011.

Calvin, William H. *A Brief History of the Mind: From Apes to Intellect and Beyond.* New York: Oxford University Press, 2004.

Capra, Fritjof. *The Tao of Physics: An Exploration of the Parallels Between Modern Physics and Eastern Mysticism.* Berkeley; [New York]: Shambhala ; distributed in the United States by Random House, 1975.

Childs, Christopher. *The Spirit's Terrain: Creativity, Activism, and Transformation.* Boston: Beacon Press, 1998.

Combs, Allan. *Consciousness Explained Better: Towards an Integral Understanding of the Multifaceted Nature of Consciousness.* St. Paul, MN: Paragon House, 2009.

Davies, P. C. W. *The Cosmic Blueprint.* London: Heinemann, 1987.

Davis, Mike. *Ecology of Fear: Los Angeles and the Imagination of Disaster.* New York: Metropolitan Books, 1998.

Diamond, Jared M. *Collapse: How Societies Choose to Fail or Succeed.* New York: Viking, 2005.

———. *Guns, Germs, and Steel: The Fates of Human Societies.* New York: W.W. Norton & Co., 1998.

Doidge, Norman. *The Brain That Changes Itself: Stories of Personal Triumph from the Frontiers of Brain Science.* New York: Viking, 2007.

Douglas-Klotz, Neil. *The Hidden Gospel: Decoding the Spiritual Message of the Aramaic Jesus.* Wheaton, IL: Quest Books, Theosophical Pub. House, 1999.

Duhm, Dieter. *The Sacred Matrix: From the Matrix of Violence to the Matrix of Life: The Foundation for a New Civilization.* Wiesenburg: Meiga, 2006.

Edelman, Gerald M. *Second Nature: Brain Science and Human Knowledge.* New Haven: Yale University Press, 2006.

Edwards, Andres R. and David Orr. *The Sustainability Revolution: Portrait of a Paradigm Shift.* Gabriola, BC: New Society Publishers, 2005.

Ehrman, Bart D. *Misquoting Jesus: The Story Behind Who Changed the Bible and Why.* New York: HarperSanFrancisco, 2005.

Elgin, Duane. *Living Universe.* San Francisco: Berrett-Koehler Publishers, Incorporated, 2009. https://ezproxy.siast.sk.ca:443/login?url=http://proquest.safaribooksonline.com/9781576759882.

Ferris, Timothy. *Coming of Age in the Milky Way.* New York: Morrow, 1988.

Flannery, Tim F. *The Weather Makers: How Man Is Changing the Climate and What It Means for Life on Earth.* New York: Atlantic Monthly Press, 2005.

Forest, Ohky Simine. *Dreaming the Council Ways: True Native Teachings from the Red Lodge.* Red Wheel / Weiser, 2009.

George, Demetra. *Mysteries of the Dark Moon: The Healing Power of the Dark Goddess.* San Francisco: HarperSanFrancisco, 1992.

Hansen, James E. *Storms of My Grandchildren: The Truth About the Coming Climate Catastrophe and Our Last Chance to Save Humanity.* New York: Bloomsbury USA, 2009.

Hartmann, Thom. *Screwed: The Undeclared War Against the Middle Class—and What We Can Do About It.* San Francisco: Berrett-Koehler Publishers, 2006.

———. *The Last Hours of Ancient Sunlight: Waking up to Personal and Global Transformation.* New York: Harmony Books, 1999.

Hawken, Paul. *Blessed Unrest: How the Largest Movement in the World Came into Being, and Why No One Saw It Coming.* New York: Viking, 2007.

Hedges, Chris. *Empire of Illusion: The End of Literacy and the Triumph of Spectacle.* New York: Nation Books, 2009.

Humphrey, Nicholas. *A History of the Mind.* New York: Simon & Schuster, 1992.

International Forum on Globalization., Cavanagh. *Alternatives to Economic Globalization.* San Francisco: Berrett-Koehler, 2002.

Jackson, Tim. *Prosperity Without Growth: Economics for a Finite Planet.* London; Sterling, VA: Earthscan, 2009.

Kasser, Rodolphe. *The Gospel of Judas: From Codex Tchacos.* Washington, DC: National Geographic, 2006.

Ken Carey. *The Third Millennium,* n.d.

Khanna, Parag. *How to Run the World: Charting a Course to the Next Renaissance.* New York: Random House, 2011.

Kolbert, Elizabeth. *Field Notes from a Catastrophe: Man, Nature, and Climate Change.* New York: Bloomsbury Pub. : Distributed to the trade by Holtzbrinck Publishers, 2006.

Korten, David C. *The Great Turning: From Empire to Earth Community.* San Francisco; Bloomfield, CT: Berrett-Koehler; Kumarian Press, 2006.

Krosney, Herbert. *The Lost Gospel: The Quest for the Gospel of Judas Iscariot.* Washington, DC: National Geographic, 2006.

Lipton, Bruce H. *The Biology of Belief: Unleashing the Power of Consciousness, Matter, and Miracles*. Santa Rosa, CA: Mountain of Love/Elite Books, 2005.

Lovelock, James. *The Vanishing Face of Gaia: a Final Warning*. New York: Basic Books, 2009.

Lovins, Amory B. *Reinventing Fire: Bold Business Solutions for the New Energy Era*. White River Junction, VT: Chelsea Green Pub., 2011.

Macy, Joanna. *Coming Back to Life: Practices to Reconnect Our Lives, Our World*. Gabriola Island, BC; Stony Creek, CT: New Society Publishers, 1998.

————. *The Work That Reconnects*. Gabriola Island, BC: New Society Publishers, 2006.

Marcus, Gary F. *The Birth of the Mind: How a Tiny Number of Genes Creates the Complexities of Human Thought*. New York: Basic Books, 2004.

McIntosh, Steve. *Integral Consciousness and the Future of Evolution*. Paragon House, 2007.

McKibben, Bill. *Deep Economy: The Wealth of Communities and the Durable Future*. New York: Times Books, 2007.

————. *Eaarth*. New York: Time Books/Henry Holt, 2010.

————. *The End of Nature*. New York: Random House, 1989.

McTaggart, Lynne. *The Field: The Quest for the Secret Force of the Universe*. Updated. Harper Perennial, 2008.

Mehl-Madrona, Lewis. *Narrative Medicine: The Use of History and Story in the Healing Process*. Original. Bear & Company, 2007.

Metzner, Ralph. *The Expansion of Consciousness*. Berkeley, CA: Green Earth Foundation & Regent Press, 2008.

Miller, Tyson. *Dream of a Nation: Inspiring Ideas for a Better America*. Asheville, NC: See Innovation, 2011.

Morton, Oliver. *Eating the Sun: How Plants Power the Planet*. Reprint. Harper Perennial, 2009.

Narby, Jeremy. *The Cosmic Serpent: DNA and the Origins of Knowledge*. New York: Jeremy P. Tarcher/Putnam, 1998.

Nelson, Melissa K. *Original Instructions: Indigenous Teachings for a Sustainable Future*. Rochester, VT: Bear & Company, 2008.

Orr, David W. *Down to the Wire: Confronting Climate Collapse*. Oxford; New York: Oxford University Press, 2009.

———. *Hope Is an Imperative: The Essential David Orr*. Washington, DC: Island Press, 2010. http://site.ebrary.com/id/10430950.

Pogacnik, Marko. *Christ Power and the Earth Goddess*. Chicago: Findhorn Press, 1999. url=http://www.msvu.eblib.com/patron/FullRecord.aspx..

Powell, Diane Hennacy. *The ESP Enigma: The Scientific Case for Psychic Phenomena*. New York: Walker, 2009.

Radin, Dean I. *The Conscious Universe: The Scientific Truth of Psychic Phenomena*. New York: HarperEdge, 1997.

Rifkin, Jeremy. *The Empathic Civilization: The Race to Global Consciousness in a World in Crisis*. New York: J.P. Tarcher/Penguin, 2009.

Roberts, Paul. *The End of Oil: On the Edge of a Perilous New World*. Boston: Houghton Mifflin, 2004.

Rosenblum, Bruce, and Fred Kuttner. *Quantum Enigma: Physics Encounters Consciousness*. 2nd ed. Oxford University Press, USA, 2011.

Sagan, Carl. *Pale Blue Dot: a Vision of the Human Future in Space*. New York: Random House, 1994.

Sahtouris, Elisabet. *Gaia: The Human Journey from Chaos to Cosmos.* New York: Pocket Books, 1989.

Shlain, Leonard. *Sex, Time, and Power: How Women's Sexuality Shaped Human Evolution.* New York: Viking, 2003.

———. *The Alphabet Versus the Goddess: The Conflict Between Word and image.* New York: Viking, 1998.

Speth. J. G. *The Bridge at the Edge of the World: Capitalism, the Environment, and Crossing from Crisis to Sustainability.* New Haven: Yale University Press, 2008.

Swimme, Brian. *The Powers of the Universe.* C enter for the Story of the Universe, 2004.

Voth, Grant L. *Myth in Human History.* Chantilly, VA: Teaching Co., 2010.

Walker, Evan Harris. *The Physics of Consciousness: The Quantum Minds and the Meaning of Life.* Cambridge: Perseus Books, 2000.

Wikman, Monika. *Pregnant Darkness: Alchemy and the Rebirth of Consciousness.* Berwick, ME; York Beach, ME: Nicolas-Hays ; Distributed to the trade by Red Wheel/Weiser, 2004.

Wilber, Ken. *A Brief History of Everything.* Boston: Shambhala, 1996.

Wright, Robert. *The Moral Animal: Evolutionary Psychology and Everyday Life.* New York: Vintage Books, 1995.

Zajonc, Arthur. *Catching the Light: The Entwined History of Light and Mind.* New York: Bantam Books, 1993.

Zimmer, Carl. *Soul Made Flesh: The Discovery of the Brain—and How It Changed the World.* New York: Free Press, 2004.

Made in the USA
San Bernardino, CA
24 September 2014